bread
butter
bottled water
beer
soft drinks
tablecloth
table-clips for cloth
napkins
paper towel
moist wipes
plastic bags *
wrapping foil
rug and cushions
folding table and chairs
balloons *
first aid kit
freezer packs (frozen in advance)
--

For Barbecues

barbecue
charcoal
lighter fuel
water spray
tongs
oven gloves

* see Hints on page 89

PERFECT
PICNICS

Foreword

This book began by the purest chance at a cricket match in the country on a summer's day. Our village team from Charlton, in Wiltshire, was playing the Heartaches, a roving team raised and led by the lyricist Tim Rice. My publisher, Colin Webb, and his wife Pamela, came down to watch and to share in the buffet lunch we always lay on for the visitors beforehand. Colin enjoyed the lunch. He seemed to enjoy the tea even more. Three pieces of Mary's lemon syrup cake disappeared with no trouble at all. What I think he liked was the apparently casual way everything that day was planned and cooked at home in our own kitchen.

Mary and our daughter Debbie had never written a cook book before. Since then they have spent the best part of a year cooking, testing, tasting, trying again and gradually refining their views until the book was done. You will hardly expect a disinterested view from me; but having had the good luck to have a preview of just about everything in it, I believe they have put together a first cookery book that is remarkable for its originality and honesty, its simplicity and its flair.

I will not say they have always been easy to live with while the book was going through its long gestation. They are both perfectionists, and they wanted to write a book that would be as thorough, exact and helpful in its recipes as possible. I believe they have translated and expanded the delights of that summer's day into a prospectus of cooking pleasures everybody can enjoy all year round. I am sure you will agree.

Godfrey Smith

PERFECT PICNICS

M A R Y   A N D   D E B B I E   S M I T H

PAVILION

FOR GODDERS
AN IDEAL MAN AT A PICNIC

First published in Great Britain in 1993 by
PAVILION BOOKS LIMITED
26 Upper Ground, London SE1 9PD

Text copyright © Mary Smith and Debbie Smith 1993
Illustrations copyright © Julia Bigg 1993

Designed by Janet James

A CIP catalogue record for this book is available from
the British Library

ISBN 1 85145 744 5

Printed and bound in Italy by L.E.G.O.

2 4 6 8 10 9 7 5 3 1

Notes on the Recipes
Stock: Good quality stock (bouillon) cubes can be used.
Eggs: Young children, the elderly, invalids and pregnant
women should avoid recipes with uncooked eggs.
Egg sizes: Small egg UK 4 or 5/US large or medium; Medium egg
UK 3/US large; Large egg UK 1 or 2/US jumbo or extra large.
Metric conversions are approximate; use either imperial
or metric measurements throughout a recipe.
1 tbsp = 15ml; 1 tsp = 5ml.

CONTENTS

Introduction

The English have a perverse and God-given gift for picnics. When we consider the draughty and windswept little island that forms the backdrop to all English picnics, it is little short of miraculous that they should be such a quintessentially English thing. This book is an attempt to capture the essence of English picnics in a practical way, taking you all through the year: through the rigours of the car park festivities for an international rugby match at Twickenham, to a romantic summer picnic and from a robust autumn barbecue at Guy Fawkes or Hallowe'en to a celebration of carol singing at Christmas.

Everything we offer here has been tested and tried in its natural place in the long cycle of the English year. We hope it will be found to have new ideas, but ideas that are entirely practical and easy to make. We like to believe that *Perfect Picnics* will give everyone who loves the special delights and hazards of outdoor feasting a down-to-earth basis for new dishes: new presentations, as it were, of a singular and enduring English pleasure.

Mary Smith
Debbie Smith

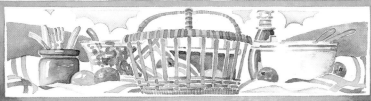

SIMPLE SPRING PICNIC

MENU FOR 12

Leek, Carrot and Potato Soup

Wholemeal (Whole-wheat) Rolls

Chicken Drumsticks Baked in Honey

Sausage and Egg Loaf in Pastry

Pasta, Tuna and Anchovy Salad

Crunchy Salad on Skewers

Lemon Syrup Cake

A combination for any occasion that should appeal to children as well as adults.

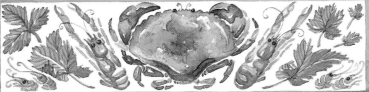

LEEK, CARROT AND POTATO SOUP

SERVES 12

50g / 2oz / 4 tbsp butter
1.3kg / 3lb leeks, trimmed, sliced in
half lengthways, then chopped
and rinsed
750g / 1½lb / 5 cups carrots, peeled
and sliced
450g / 1lb / 3 cups potatoes, peeled
and cut into chunks
1.8 litres / 3 pints / 7½ cups
chicken stock
salt and freshly ground black pepper
900ml / 1½ pints / 3¾ cups milk
chopped fresh parsley or chives,
to serve
150ml / 5fl oz / ⅔ cup single (light)
cream (optional)

This soup is one of our perennial favourites, an English variant on *potage parmentier*. Use a very large, heavy-based saucepan, that will hold 4½ litres / 9 pints / 5½ quarts.

Melt the butter in a large, heavy-based saucepan. Add all the vegetables, stirring with a wooden spoon so they are evenly coated with the butter, then cover and leave the vegetables to sweat for about 5 minutes over very low heat. Pour in half the stock, stir well and season with salt and pepper. Bring the soup to the boil, then reduce the heat and simmer for about 25 minutes, or until the vegetables are tender.

Purée the soup in a food processor or blender until smooth; this may have to be done in several batches. Return the puréed soup to the pan. Add the rest of the stock and the milk, stir well and bring it almost back to the boil. Check the seasoning and sprinkle on the parsley or chives before serving.

For an extra-rich soup, stir in a little cream as well.

WHOLEMEAL (WHOLE-WHEAT) ROLLS

MAKES 12

1 quantity Wholemeal (whole-
wheat) Bread with sunflower seeds
(page 73)
milk for glazing
seeds, such as poppy, sesame,
sunflower or caraway, or porridge
oats, or extra flour

You will need a well-greased loaf tin (bread pan) that measures about 19 × 24 × 5cm / 7½ × 9½ × 2in.

Make the wholemeal (whole-wheat) bread dough (on page 73), leaving out the sunflower seeds. After the dough has risen and doubled in size for the first time, process or knead it again lightly. Divide the dough into 12 even-sized portions and roll each one into a smooth ball. Place them in rows in the tin (pan) and cover with a cloth, then leave the rolls in a warm place to rise again for a further 30 minutes. Meanwhile, preheat the oven to 230°C / 450°F / Gas Mark 8.

Brush the rolls with a little milk, then spinkle a few seeds such as poppy, sesame, sunflower, caraway or porridge oats or a little flour. Bake for about 30 minutes, until the rolls sound hollow if tapped on the bottom, then turn them out on to a wire rack to cool.

CHICKEN DRUMSTICKS BAKED IN HONEY

SERVES 12

Corn oil
30 large chicken drumsticks
3-4 tbsp soy (soya) sauce
6-8 tbsp runny honey
2 tsp dry mustard powder
juice of 2 lemons

Drumsticks are so easy to pick up and eat at a picnic that they are always very popular, so allow at least two drumsticks per person. We put foil round the ends once they are cool, as they are rather sticky.

Preheat the oven to 200°C / 400°F / Gas Mark 6. Brush the base and sides of a roasting tin (pan) large enough to take the drumsticks in a single layer with oil. Prick the skin of the drumsticks all over with a skewer. Mix the soy (soya) sauce, honey, mustard and half the lemon juice together in a bowl. Place the drumsticks in the roasting pan in a single layer, then coat them with about half the honey mixture. Bake the drumsticks for 30 minutes, then turn them over and coat the other side with the remaining honey mixture. Bake for a further 15 minutes. Dribble on the rest of the lemon juice and cover with foil and cook for another 15 minutes, or until the meat juices run clear when tested with the tip of a knife inserted in the thickest part. Ease the drumsticks free with a fish slice (pancake turner) if they stick to the base of the pan and place on a dish to cool.

SAUSAGE AND EGG LOAF IN PASTRY

SERVES 12

2 × 225g/8oz packets (packages)
puff pastry (dough), thawed
if frozen
milk or beaten egg, for glaze

FOR THE FILLING
15g/½oz/1 tbsp butter
½ tbsp oil
1 onion, peeled and finely chopped
225g/8oz chicken or turkey livers,
discoloured sections cut off, trimmed
and roughly chopped
1 tbsp dried mixed herbs
(Italian seasoning)
2 small Cox's Orange Pippin or
other eating apples, peeled, cored
and grated
salt and freshly ground black pepper
1.3kg/3lb pork sausage-meat
6 small eggs, hard-boiled (hard-
cooked) and shelled

This large scale, slightly sophisticated version of a traditional British sausage roll contains a surprise egg and was loved by our children when small. The following recipe makes two loaves. Sausage-meat is usually quite highly seasoned, so it should not need any additional salt and pepper. If you are not sure about the seasoning, fry a little piece of the sausage-meat, allow it to cool and then taste it.

Preheat the oven to 220°C / 425°F / Gas Mark 7. To make the filling, melt the butter with the oil in a frying pan (skillet). Fry the onion for 2-3 minutes, or until golden, then turn up the heat and add the livers. Cook them quickly, stirring continuously, for about 3 minutes, until they are firm but still a little pink in the centres. Cool. Mix the onion, livers, herbs, apples and any seasoning into the sausage-meat. Roll out half the pastry dough on a lightly floured surface to a rectangle about 30 × 35cm / 12 × 14in. Place the pastry dough on a baking (cookie) sheet. Arrange one quarter of the meat mixture down the centre, leaving clear edges of about 6.25cm/2½in at each end and about 10cm/4in along the sides. Place 3 eggs on top of the sausage-meat in a row. Slightly flatten out a second quarter of the meat mixture and cover the eggs with it. Shape the meat mixture into a fairly even sausage.

14

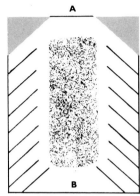

Using the point of a sharp knife, cut incisions in the pastry dough at approximately 2.5cm /1in intervals in a herringbone design, as shown in the sketch. Cut away the 2 triangles which have been shaded along side A. Turn the pastry flap along side B over the back of the loaf and brush it with milk or beaten egg. Criss-cross the strips, starting from side A, across the back of the loaf to side B. Press the strips down lightly, then brush the whole loaf with milk or beaten egg. The pastry may not appear very neat at this stage but once it has risen and browned the effect will be quite impressive. Repeat the process with the second loaf. Bake both loaves for 40 minutes, or until risen and golden brown. Allow to cool.

PASTA, TUNA AND ANCHOVY SALAD

SERVES 12

450g / 1lb pasta bows or shells
450g / 1lb / 2²/₃ cups sweetcorn
kernels (whole kernel corn),
drained if canned and cooked,
drained and cooled if frozen
2 × 400g / 14oz cans red kidney
beans, well drained and rinsed
2 × 200g / 7oz cans tuna, drained
and flaked
1 × 50g / 1³/₄oz can anchovy fillets,
drained and chopped
3 tbsp capers, drained
1 bunch spring onions (scallions),
trimmed and chopped
3 green peppers, cored, de-seeded,
rinsed and diced

FOR THE DRESSING
300ml / ¹/₂ pint / 1¹/₄ cups good-
quality mayonnaise
300ml / ¹/₂ pint / 1¹/₄ cups
plain yogurt
75ml / 3fl oz / 6 tbsp olive oil
1 tbsp lemon juice
1 tbsp chopped fresh thyme
or 1 tsp dried
2 tbsp chopped fresh parsley
1 small clove garlic, peeled and very
finely chopped
salt and freshly ground black pepper

This salad can be eaten straight away, but its flavours improve after several hours.

Cook the pasta according to the instructions on the packet (package) then drain well and put it in a large bowl with the rest of the salad ingredients while the pasta is still warm, but not hot. Combine the dressing ingredients or shake them in a screw-top jar and pour over the salad, mixing together thoroughly. Cover until ready to serve at room temperature.

CRUNCHY SALAD ON SKEWERS

green, red or yellow peppers, cored, seeded and cut into chunks
cherry tomatoes, wiped and skewered whole
cucumber, cut lengthways and then into chunks
cauliflower florets (flowerets) blanched and broken into small sprigs
radishes, wiped, topped and tailed
baby corn lightly blanched
celery trimmed and cut into pieces

A useful way of serving a crunchy salad at a picnic with special appeal to children is to prepare individual skewers threaded with any of the ingredients on the left.

Allow 1 skewer per person. For easy transport, wrap each skewer in foil, or pack them together in a suitable plastic box with lid. Take a jar of dressing, as for Garlicky Green Salad on page 24, omitting the garlic, to dip the skewered salad into.

LEMON SYRUP CAKE

SERVES 6-8

make 2 cakes for 12 people

FOR THE CAKE
*175g / 6oz / 1½ cups self-raising
(self-rising) flour
1 tsp baking powder
175g / 6oz / scant 1 cup caster
(superfine) sugar
175g / 6oz / 12 tbsp butter, softened,
plus a little extra
3 medium eggs
finely grated rind (peel) and 1 tbsp
juice from 1 lemon*

FOR THE SYRUP
*100g / 4oz / ½ cup caster
(superfine) sugar
3 tbsp lemon juice*

For a deep 20cm / 8in cake tin (pan).

Preheat the oven to 180°C / 350°F / Gas Mark 4. Melt a little butter and brush the cake tin (pan) with it. Line the base and sides with greaseproof (waxed) paper, then brush the paper with melted butter. Sift the flour and baking powder together and put them in a food processor. Add the sugar, butter, eggs, lemon rind (peel) and juice and process until smooth.

Alternatively, sift the flour and baking powder into a mixing bowl, then beat in the remaining ingredients until smooth. Put the mixture into the tin and level the surface. Bake for 1 hour, covering it with a piece of foil for the last 15 minutes if it seems to be getting too brown.

Meanwhile, stir the remaining sugar and lemon juice in a small saucepan over medium heat until the sugar melts, then let it simmer to make a syrup. As soon as the cake is out of the oven, prick the surface all over with a fork or skewer and pour the syrup on evenly. Leave the cake in the tin until it is cool.

FESTIVE SPRING PICNIC

MENU FOR 12

Game Terrine with Vine (Grape) Leaves

Crab Tarts with Calvados

Garlicky Green Salad

New Potatoes with Dill

Caramel Oranges

This rather luxurious menu is ideal for a picnic at a horse race meeting, such as the Cheltenham Gold Cup, which takes place each March. The quantities can easily be adapted for fewer people. In which case, make the game terrine in two or three smaller dishes, cook and freeze whatever is not used.

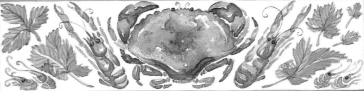

GAME TERRINE WITH
VINE (GRAPE) LEAVES

SERVES 12

*1 pheasant, skinned, sinews and
bones removed and cut into
small pieces
450g / 1lb stewing venison, trimmed
and cut into small pieces
25g / 1oz / 2 tbsp butter
1 onion, peeled and chopped
550g / 1¼lb lean belly of pork (pork
belly), minced (ground)
100g / 4oz pork fat, minced (ground)
225g / 8oz turkey livers, trimmed
(discoloured parts removed)
and chopped
2 medium eggs
1 tbsp chopped fresh thyme or
1½ tsp dried
2 tsp salt
2 tbsp preserved green peppercorns,
well drained
12 stuffed green olives, halved
225g / 8oz packet (package)
preserved vine (grape) leaves, see
method to prepare*

Frozen game is now easy to find all the year round and therefore a game terrine is a good starter (appetizer) at any time. Buy the venison in big chunks so all the fat and gristle can be trimmed away more easily. The terrine looks very attractive in a round, shallow dish; We use one 27.5cm /11in across and 5cm / 2in deep. The capacity of the dish is 2.4 litres / 4 pints / 2½ quarts. The method of preparing vine (grape) leaves is very well described by Claudia Roden in *A Book of Middle Eastern Food*, and is as follows: If using vine leaves preserved in brine, put them in a large bowl and pour boiling water over them. Make sure the water penetrates well between the layers and allow the leaves to soak for 20 minutes. Drain. Soak in fresh cold water for a further 20 minutes, then drain again and repeat the process once more. This will remove excess salt. If using fresh young vine leaves, soften them by plunging three or four at a time in boiling water for a few minutes until they become limp.

Serve sliced with Wholemeal (Whole-wheat) Bread with Sunflower Seeds (page 73) and redcurrant jelly or Cumberland Sauce (page 44).

Put all the marinade ingredients in a dish with the pheasant and venison and leave them in a cool place for 24 hours, stirring occasionally.

Preheat the oven to 160°C / 325°F / Gas Mark 3. Melt the butter and fry the onion until softened, but not browned. Put it in a large dish with the belly of pork (pork belly), pork fat, turkey livers, eggs, thyme, salt and green peppercorns, mixing them together thoroughly. Remove the pheasant and venison from the marinade with a slotted spoon, then strain and reserve the marinade, discarding bay leaves, onion and mace. Mix 3 tbsp of the marinade into the minced (ground) meat mixture.

FOR THE MARINADE
300ml / ½ pint / 1½ cups port
2 bay leaves
1 onion, peeled and stuck with
7 cloves
1 mace blade

Press each individual vine leaf between pieces of absorbent kitchen paper (paper towels) to dry, then line the terrine dish, allowing part of the leaves to overhang the edge and keeping some aside for the top. Put half the meat mixture in the base of the lined dish, spreading it fairly evenly and dot with the olives. Arrange the pheasant and venison on top, then another layer of the meat mixture. Cover the top surface with vine leaves, folding in any that overhang the edge.

Put a piece of buttered foil over the terrine and bake for 2½ hours in a *bain marie* by putting the dish in a roasting pan with enough boiling water to reach halfway up the terrine's sides. Check the water level in the pan from time to time. Uncover the terrine and leave it to cool, then cover it again with foil. Put even pressure on it with weights while refrigerating it overnight. Turn the terrine out on to a large plate, pouring off any excess juices.

CRAB TARTS WITH CALVADOS

SERVES 12

Use twelve 10cm/4in round fluted tart tins (pans) with removable bases

FOR THE PASTRY
*450g/1lb/4 cups plain white
(all-purpose) flour
225g/8oz/2 sticks butter
1 medium egg
about 1 tbsp cold water*

FOR THE FILLING
*1 tbsp olive oil
4-6 crabs
juice of 1 lemon
salt and freshly ground black pepper
600ml/1 pint/2½ cups single
(light) cream
125ml/4fl oz/½ cup Calvados
48 Dublin Bay prawns
(langoustines), to decorate
fresh chopped parsley, to decorate*

Our neighbour, Ian MacArthur, has persuaded us that dealing with crabs is not as awesome as we feared. His simple but delicious recipe for crab with Calvados is good served hot or cold. Crabs are usually bought cooked and are readily available from good fishmongers. When choosing the crab, shake it slightly, as it should feel heavy but there should not be a sound of water inside. Crabs vary enormously in size but for this dish a total of 3.6kg/8lb bought weight will be sufficient. This means you will require 4-6 crabs.

To extract the meat, first twist off the legs and the two main claws near the head. Place the body of the crab on a chopping board. With the head away from you, push the soft body out of the shell with your thumbs and carefully prise it away so it comes out completely intact. The stomach sac, which is rather similar to a poultry gizzard, is found directly behind the mouth and must be removed as well as the feathery gills. These are not edible. Cut the hard inner body in half lengthways with a sharp knife and pick out all the meat from the crevices with a skewer or a two-pronged pick. Remove any meat left in the main shell with a teaspoon and put all the meat, brown, white and orange-red, in a large bowl. Break the legs at the joints and extract the meat with a skewer or pick. To crack the main claws, hold the joints in the palm of your hand and tap the shell with a mallet or rolling pin. Get the crab meat out with your fingers or the handle of a teaspoon, discarding the flat bone. Look out for fragments of shell.

For the picnic, transport the baked pastry cases in their tins (pans) with the prepared crab mixture and Dublin Bay prawns (langoustines) packed separately in sealed containers. Keep the crab mixture and Dublin Bay prawns (langoustine) in a cooling box with freezer packs. To assemble, take the pastry cases out of their tins and fill each on site with the crab mixture. Decorate with the Dublin Bay prawns (langoustines) and parsley.

Make the pastry dough as for Leek and Broccoli Flan (Quiche) (page 70) and chill for about 30 minutes. Preheat the oven to 200°C / 400°F / Gas Mark 6.

Divide the pastry dough into 12 pieces and line each individual tart tin (pan). Prick the bases with a fork and bake blind (see Leek and Broccoli Flan (Quiche) on page 70) for 10 minutes. Then remove the greaseproof (waxed) paper and beans and continue cooking for a further 5 minutes. Leave to cool in the tins on a wire rack.

Put the olive oil in a large, heavy-based frying pan (skillet), shake the pan to coat the base and sides and warm the oil on a medium heat for 1-2 minutes. Add the crab meat and warm it through, turning it gently with a wooden spoon. Add the lemon juice and salt and pepper, then pour the cream and half the Calvados over the crab meat and reheat, stirring gently. Dribble the remaining Calvados over the mixture and set alight. Allow to flame for a few moments. Serve immediately or leave to cool completely and assemble as above.

GARLICKY GREEN SALAD

SERVES 12

*1 large or 2 small heads Iceberg
lettuce, or other crisp green leaf
salad, rinsed and torn into
small pieces
2 bunches fresh watercress, well
rinsed, thick stalks (stems) removed
and broken into sprigs
100g / 4oz mange-touts (snow peas),
rinsed, topped and tailed
100g / 4oz French (green) beans,
rinsed, topped and tailed
200g / 8oz / 1⅓ cups broccoli florets
(flowerets), rinsed
1 small cucumber, cut lengthways,
rinsed and sliced
2 green peppers, rinsed, cored,
de-seeded and sliced
225g / 8oz seedless green grapes,
rinsed*

FOR THE DRESSING
*300ml / 10fl oz / 1¼ cups
good-quality olive oil
2 tbsp white wine vinegar
1 heaped tbsp coarse-grain mustard
2 large cloves garlic, peeled and very
finely chopped
salt and freshly ground black pepper*

All the salad ingredients, which must be viewed as approximate amounts, can be prepared in advance and stored in a plastic bag in the refrigerator or cooling box. Arrange them in a bowl and pour the dressing on about 30 minutes before serving.

Blanche the mange-touts (snow peas) by putting them in lightly salted boiling water just until the water returns to the boil, then draining immediately. Steam the beans, using a metal colander over a saucepan if you do not have a steamer, for 3-5 minutes, until slightly tender but still crunchy. Steam the broccoli florets (flowerets) for 7-9 minutes, until just lightly cooked. Plunge all the vegetables into cold water as soon as they are tender, then drain them well. Combine the salad leaves and all the vegetables in a large bowl. Mix the dressing ingredients together well or shake them in a screw-top jar and pour over the salad.

NEW POTATOES WITH DILL

Cook the potatoes as described for the festive summer menu (page 30) but omit the sprig of mint. Rinse the dill, cut away the main stalks and chop it finely. Add a generous amount of chopped dill to the warm potatoes with the butter.

CARAMEL ORANGES

SERVES 12

18 oranges
10 tbsp brandy
350g / 12oz / 1¾ cups caster
(superfine) sugar
30ml / 2 tbsp water

With a pointed, sharp knife mark out the orange skin in quarters, then peel carefully, removing all the bitter white pith. Reserve the rind (peel) from 2 oranges. Cut the oranges fairly thinly into horizontal slices, then lay them on a shallow dish, taking care to remove all the pips (seeds). Dribble the brandy evenly over the oranges. Cut away the white inner skin from the reserved rind and snip the rind with a pair of scissors into very fine strips, about 3cm / ⅛in wide. Put the rind in a saucepan with cold water to cover and bring to the boil. Drain it and plunge the rind into cold water. This will remove the bitter taste. Drain again and

return the rind to the saucepan with fresh cold water to cover. Simmer for 10-12 minutes, until tender. Drain again and put aside.

To make the caramel syrup, put the sugar and water in a heavy-based frying pan (skillet) and dissolve the sugar over medium heat, stirring continuously with a wooden spoon. The sugar and water will initially have a sticky consistency but, after a few minutes the sugar will dissolve and form a thickish brown syrup. Add the orange rind strips, coat them on all sides with the wooden spoon and simmer for 1-2 minutes, until glazed. Spoon the syrup and rind strips evenly over the oranges. The syrup will initially caramelize, but if left overnight, it will liquify, which may be preferable.

FESTIVE SUMMER PICNIC

MENU FOR 12

Parma Ham (Prosciutto) and Melon

Layered Salmon Wrapped in Spinach Leaves

Warm New Potatoes with Mint

Paule's Salad

Hazelnut Flan (Sponge) with Summer Fruit and

Strawberry Sauce

Long summer days lend themselves to festive picnics or entertaining at Henley or Ascot. The trick is to avoid the obvious, such as cold salmon and mayonnaise or rare roast beef. Here are ideas for an unexpected, yet memorable, alfresco meal.

PARMA HAM (PROSCIUTTO) AND MELON

Allow about 50g / 2oz Parma ham (prosciutto) per person and ⅓-½ Galia melon or similar. Parma ham must be paper-thin and ideally should be freshly cut. In England, however, where the demand is not heavy we have found packs of Parma ham from Marks and Spencer hard to beat.

Freshly ground black pepper is essential with Parma ham, so take a pepper-mill to the picnic. Arrange the Parma ham on a flat dish, cover it well and transport in an insulated cool bag, keeping the dish horizontal. The melon needs to be de-seeded and is easier to handle unpeeled. Cut it into thin slices, then re-assemble it, wrap in foil and keep cool until needed.

LAYERED SALMON WRAPPED IN SPINACH LEAVES

SERVES 12

*about 25g / 1oz / 2 tbsp butter, melted
1kg / 2¼lb fresh salmon in 1 piece,
preferably a middle cut
1 lemon, rind (peel) grated,
then sliced
450g / 1lb large spinach leaves,
well rinsed and tough stalks
(stems) removed
450g / 1lb fresh haddock, skinned,
filleted and roughly chopped
300ml / ½ pint / 1¼ cups double
(heavy) cream
300ml / ½ pint / 1¼ cups sour cream
6 medium eggs
2-3 tbsp chopped fresh dill
freshly grated nutmeg
salt and freshly ground black pepper*

For two 900g / 2lb loaf tins (bread pans) that measure about 21 × 11 × 6.25cm / 8¼ × 4¼ × 2½in, or 2 cast-iron pâté terrines with lids, about 25 × 10cm / 10 × 4in.

Preheat the oven to 180°C / 350°F / Gas Mark 4. Brush a large piece of foil with melted butter and place the salmon in the centre. Arrange the lemon slices inside and on top of the salmon together with some seasoning. Scrunch the edges of foil together to seal the fish, put it on a baking (cookie) sheet and bake it for 45 minutes. Leave in the foil until cool. Chill the salmon in the refrigerator, then skin and fillet it, taking care to remove any small bones. Divide each salmon fillet in half/lengthways and put the 4 pieces aside.

Put the spinach leaves in a colander and pour over a kettleful of boiling water, then leave the spinach to drain very well. Generously grease the tins (pans) with butter then line them with the spinach leaves, leave part of the leaves overlapping the edge and keeping some aside for the top.

Preheat the oven to 180°C / 350°F / Gas Mark 4. Process the haddock in a food processor or blender until completely smooth, then add the double (heavy) cream, sour cream, eggs, dill, lemon rind (peel), some

nutmeg and seasoning and process again to combine. Alternatively, mince (grind) the haddock, then stir in the sour cream, eggs, dill, lemon rind, nutmeg and seasoning and mix together thoroughly. Put one-quarter of the white fish mixture into the bottom of one lined tin (pan). Place 2 pieces of salmon on top to make a salmon layer, then cover the salmon with another one-quarter of the white fish mixture. Repeat with the second tin.

Cover each tin with the remaining spinach, folding over any overhanging leaves. Place a piece of wet greaseproof (waxed) paper on top and bake in a *bain marie* by putting the loaf tins in a roasting pan with enough boiling water to reach about halfway up the sides of the tins. Bake for 45 minutes or until a skewer inserted into the white fish mixture comes out clean. Leave to cool in the tins before turning out. Chill in the refrigerator.

WARM NEW POTATOES WITH MINT

New English potatoes cooked with a sprig of fresh mint are perfect to serve with the cold salmon.

For a picnic, scrub the potatoes in advance. Cook them at the last minute in a heavy-based saucepan with a tight-fitting lid, just covered with lightly salted boiling water, until just tender. Drain them quickly, remove the mint and put them straight back in the hot pan with a knob of butter. Shake the potatoes gently over low heat to coat them evenly with the butter. Put the lid on the pan and wrap it well in a thick blanket. This ensures the potatoes are kept warm for the picnic.

PAULE'S SALAD

SERVES 12

FOR THE SALAD
*1-2 large Webb (Bibb), Cos
(Romaine) or similar crisp green
lettuce, outer leaves removed, rinsed
and torn into pieces
8 eggs, hard-boiled (hard-cooked)
shelled and quartered
2-3 tsp chopped fresh chives*

FOR THE DRESSING
*1 bunch spring onions (scallions)
trimmed and chopped
300ml / ½ pint / 1¼ cups sour cream
or fromage frais
salt and freshly ground black pepper*

We first tasted this salad with our old French friends, the L'Estiennes, in Honfleur, on a summer evening, and for us it evokes Proustian memories of that enchanted night. It is difficult to make the salad look very attractive, but the flavour makes up for its appearance. This can also be used as a starter (appetizer), in which case use more eggs.

Arrange the lettuce and eggs in a large, shallow dish. Stir the spring onions (scallions) and some seasoning into the sour cream or fromage frais then pour it over the salad and gently mix it all together well. Sprinkle the chives on top.

HAZELNUT FLAN (SPONGE) WITH SUMMER FRUIT AND STRAWBERRY SAUCE

SERVES 6
*make 2 flans and double the
quantities for the sauce to serve 12*

FOR THE FLAN (SPONGE)
*melted butter for greasing
75g / 3oz / ¾ cup plain white
(all-purpose) flour, sifted
75g / 3oz / ¾ cup hazelnuts, skinned
(see page 39) and finely ground
3 large eggs, at room temperature,
separated
75g / 3oz / scant ½ cup caster
(superfine) sugar
3 tbsp brandy or Armagnac*

FOR THE FILLING
*175-225g / 6-8oz / about 1 cup
caster (superfine) sugar
900g / 2lb mixed summer fruit, such
as raspberries and redcurrants,
lightly rinsed and drained*

FOR THE SAUCE
*350g / 12oz strawberries, hulled,
lightly rinsed and well drained
75-100g / 3-4oz / about ½ cup caster
(superfine) sugar
juice of ½ small lemon
juice of ½ small orange*

Assemble the flan (sponge) before leaving for a picnic or several hours before serving. Transport it on a large plate, loosely covered in foil and packed in a cool box. As most cool boxes are tall and narrow, turn the box on its side to keep the flan upright. Keep the sauce, cooled, in a separate container to serve alongside the flan.

For an indented flan (sponge) tin (pan), 23cm / 9in in diameter and 2.5cm / 1in deep.

Preheat the oven to 200°C / 400°F / Gas Mark 6. Grease the flan (sponge) tin (pan). Mix the flour and ground hazelnuts together. Beat the egg yolks and sugar together until they are pale and thick. Whisk (beat) the egg whites separately until stiff. Fold the flour and hazelnut mixture and the egg whites alternately into the yolks and sugar with a large metal spoon, then pour into the flan tin. Bake for 15 minutes, until set and golden brown. Turn out on to a wire rack and leave to cool.

Meanwhile, to make the filling, lightly mix the caster (superfine) sugar into the summer fruit and put aside. For the sauce, purée the strawberries in a food processor or blender with the sugar and lemon and orange juices. Sieve the purée if necessary. Assemble the flan by spooning the brandy or Armagnac evenly over the flan base. Pile the fruit into it and serve the sauce separately.

ROMANTIC
SUMMER PICNIC

MENU FOR 6

Ilsa Yardley's Black Roe with Eggs and Cream

Rare Beef in Phyllo Pastry

Godsmay Salad

Champagne Syllabub

Hazlenut Curls

Lexi's Chocolate Strawberries

A rather special combination of dishes particularly suitable for an evening at Glyndebourne or any romantic summer celebration. Quantities are for 6 or *à deux*.

ILSA YARDLEY'S BLACK ROE WITH EGGS AND CREAM

SERVES 6

9 medium eggs, hard-boiled (hard-cooked) and shelled
about 225ml/8fl oz/1 cup double (heavy) cream
plenty of freshly ground black pepper
about 200g/7oz black lumpfish roe

Our good friend Ilsa made this starter for us many years ago, and it has proved one of our most popular dishes. It can be used equally well as a dip or spread on small water biscuits (crackers) for a drinks party.

This can either be served in a large shallow dish with a layer of roe covering the egg and cream mixture or in individual ramekins which can be transported to a picnic like the Champagne Syllabub on page 38.

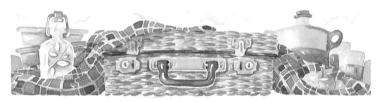

Cut the eggs in half, put the yolks in a large bowl and break them up with a fork until crumbly. Combine the yolks with the cream to make a smooth paste. Chop the egg whites finely – a potato masher is the quickest method. Mix them together with the yolk and cream mixture. Season with plenty of pepper. To serve in ramekins, divide the egg mixture among the 6 dishes. Smooth the surfaces, then put a small amount of the roe on top of each, gently spreading it over the eggs. Use up all the roe to fill any gaps. For serving in a large dish, cover all the egg mixture with roe, smoothing it evenly.

To make this for two people, use 3 medium eggs, about 75g / 3oz black lumpfish roe, about 50ml/2fl oz/¼ cup double (heavy) cream and plenty of freshly ground black pepper.

RARE BEEF IN PHYLLO PASTRY

SERVES 6

*900g / 2lb fillet of beef, trimmed and
tied (see method)
1-2 cloves garlic, peeled and cut into
slivers
50g / 2oz / 4 tbsp butter
1 tsp dried thyme
plenty of freshly ground black pepper
about 225g / 8oz phyllo pastry
dough, thawed if frozen*

The middle of the fillet is best for this dish, as it cuts into even round slices. However, an uneven end piece can be shaped into a neat roll and when tied with string will make a reasonable substitute, but is better cut into thick slices. It is most important that all the fat and sinews are trimmed from the meat and, whatever cut, the fillet should be tied with fine string in several places. Calculate a little extra weight when buying the meat to allow for the trimming.

Preheat the oven to 230°C / 450°F / Gas Mark 8. Make incisions along the length of the fillet and insert one sliver of garlic in each of them. Melt the butter in a heavy-based frying pan (skillet) and seal the meat on all sides. Sprinkle the thyme over the meat and season with pepper.

Put the meat in a roasting tin (pan) and roast for 10 minutes. Leave it to cool, then chill for 30 minutes.

Unfold the sheets of pastry and overlap the sheets forming a square

that is 10cm / 4in longer than the fillet. Brush each sheet with some of the remaining melted butter as you overlap them.

Remove the string and lay the fillet diagonally on the phyllo. Roll it up, tucking the ends into the roll. Place it on a shallow roasting pan with the join (seam) underneath and brush the surface with the rest of the butter.

Put the fillet in the oven for 20 minutes. For a less rare fillet increase the cooking time by a few minutes. Leave to cool and serve at room temperature.

To make this for two people, use two 150g / 5oz fillet steaks, 25g / 1oz / 2 tbsp butter, 1 small crushed clove garlic, a generous pinch dried thyme for each steak, plenty of freshly ground black pepper and about 50g / 2oz thawed phyllo pastry dough (2 sheets each measuring about 45 × 30cm / 18 × 12in). Press the garlic on to each side of the fillets and sprinkle them with thyme and pepper. Melt the butter in a heavy-based frying pan (skillet) and seal the steaks on both sides very briefly; reserve the rest of the butter. Chill the steaks well. Meanwhile, preheat the oven to 230°C / 450°F / Gas Mark 8.

Brush 1 sheet of phyllo pastry dough with a little of the remaining melted butter. Place a steak across one end of the sheet. Roll the steak up in the phyllo then press the pastry dough together at each side of the meat to form a Christmas cracker shape. Brush the surface all over with some more of the melted butter, then transfer it to a baking (cookie) sheet. Repeat with the second steak, then cook immediately for 10 minutes. Cool on a wire rack.

GODSMAY SALAD

SERVES 6

FOR THE SALAD
*1.8kg / 4lb fresh broad (fava) beans,
shelled, or 675g / 1½lb frozen
broad beans
1-2 bunches radishes, trimmed,
rinsed and thinly sliced
1-2 bunches watercress, well rinsed
and thick stalks (stems) removed
4 streaky bacon rashers (slices),
rinds removed if necessary, well
grilled (broiled) and cut into
small pieces
50g / 2oz / ½ cup pine nuts, toasted*

FOR THE DRESSING
*175ml / 6fl oz / ¾ cup olive oil
juice of ½ lemon
1 tbsp grainy mustard
1 tbsp runny honey
2 tbsp chopped fresh chives
salt and freshly ground black pepper*

Debbie created this salad for my husband's birthday. It contains all his favourite summer salad ingredients.

Cook the broad (fava) beans in a little salted water for 10-15 minutes or follow the instructions on the packet (package) if they are frozen. Drain them well, then put them into a dish. Meanwhile, mix together all the dressing ingredients in a screw-top jar until well combined. Pour the dressing over the beans while they are still warm. Stir in the remaining salad ingredients just before serving, reserving a few pine nuts and pieces of bacon to sprinkle on top.

To make Godsmay Salad for two people, use only a third of these quantities.

CHAMPAGNE SYLLABUB

SERVES 6

pared rind (peel) of ½ lemon
75ml / 3fl oz / about ⅓ cup
champagne
1½ tbsp lemon juice
75g / 3oz / scant ½ cup caster
(superfine) sugar
200ml / 7fl oz / scant 1 cup double
(heavy) cream

Syllabub is a very English dish dating from Elizabethan times when it was a drink made with sparkling wine and cream. In the eighteenth century, the syllabub developed into the classic English trifle by the addition of leftover sponge cake, sherry and fruit. Syllabub looks very attractive served in tall champagne glasses. For transporting to the picnic, cover each glass with foil and pack in an insulated cool box. The glasses can be protected by trimmed down cardboard dividers from an old wine box. Do not make it more than 24 hours in advance.

Reserve a little of the pared rind (peel) for decoration and put the remainder into a bowl with the champagne and lemon juice. Cover and leave overnight to infuse. Remove the rind, add the sugar and cream and whisk (beat) the mixture with an electric mixer until thick and light and the whisks leaves a trail.

Spoon the syllabub into individual glasses with a long-handled spoon. Keep in a cool place until ready to serve. To decorate it, cut the reserved rind very finely. Put it into a saucepan with a little water, bring to the boil and simmer for 2-3 minutes. Discard the water and rinse it thoroughly in cold water. Dry it on absorbent kitchen paper (paper towels) and wrap in greaseproof (waxed) paper. Sprinkle a little on top of each glass just before serving.

It does not seem worth making Champagne Syllabub for 2 people. Take champagne to drink with the Chocolate Strawberries instead.

HAZELNUT CURLS

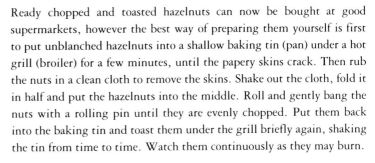

MAKES 36

100g / 4oz phyllo pastry dough,
thawed if frozen
50g / 2oz / 4 tbsp butter, melted
50g / 2oz hazelnuts, chopped and
toasted (see method)
icing (confectioners') sugar, sifted

Ready chopped and toasted hazelnuts can now be bought at good supermarkets, however the best way of preparing them yourself is first to put unblanched hazelnuts into a shallow baking tin (pan) under a hot grill (broiler) for a few minutes, until the papery skins crack. Then rub the nuts in a clean cloth to remove the skins. Shake out the cloth, fold it in half and put the hazelnuts into the middle. Roll and gently bang the nuts with a rolling pin until they are evenly chopped. Put them back into the baking tin and toast them under the grill briefly again, shaking the tin from time to time. Watch them continuously as they may burn.

Preheat the oven to 220° / 425°F / Gas Mark 7. Cut the phyllo pastry dough into strips about 8 × 15cm / 3 × 6in. Brush them all over with the butter and sprinkle about ½ tsp of nuts along each strip. Roll the phyllo strips up into a loose cigar shape and place on ungreased baking (cookie) sheets. Bake for 10 minutes. Put some icing (confectioners') sugar on to a plate and roll the hot curls in it to coat them. Leave to cool, then store in an airtight container.

LEXI'S CHOCOLATE STRAWBERRIES

SERVES 6

*225g / 8oz strawberries, preferably
about the same size
100g / 4oz bitter (bittersweet)
chocolate
12g / ½oz / 1 tbsp solid white fat
(shortening)*

We came across this delicious *bonne bouche* at the midsummer barbecue parties held in our mews off London's Portobello Road. Our neighbour, Lexi Cook, served the Chocolate Strawberries to a widely fluctuating number of people. The combination of the dark chocolate and the sweet strawberries is irresistible. You can either share a 225g / 8oz punnet of strawberries with a friend or allow three to four strawberries per person for a large gathering. These are best made and eaten on the same day. To take the strawberries on a picnic, pack them in single layers in a sealed container with a piece of foil between each layer and keep cool.

Lightly rinse the strawberries, keeping the leaves and the stalks (stems) intact and dry them well. Break up the chocolate and melt it with the fat in the top of a double saucepan or in a heatproof bowl over a pan of simmering water. Stir the mixture until it is smooth. Remove from the heat. Holding a strawberry by the stalk, dip it into the melted chocolate, coating half to two-thirds of the strawberry. Allow the excess chocolate to drip back into the saucepan. If the chocolate mixture solidifies, re-heat it gently, then continue coating the strawberries. Cover a tray with foil and place the coated strawberries on it. Leave them in the refrigerator, uncovered, to set.

SUMMER OR WINTER BUFFET

MENU FOR 25

Cold Baked Gammon (Farm Ham) with Sugar and Cloves

Cumberland Sauce

Sausages Baked in Honey and Herbs

Smoked Haddock, Leek and Tomato Flan (Quiche)

Cold Chicken with Lemon Sauce

Rice Salad with Black (Ripe) Olives

Mixed Bean Salad

Leaf Salad

Wholemeal (Whole-wheat) Orange Biscuits (Cookies)

Strawberry Ice Cream

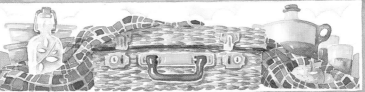

We use variations of this buffet menu on all sorts of occasions from anniversaries, birthdays and reunions to village cricket lunches.

If there are going to be an elastic number of guests, a couple of dozen hard-boiled (hard-cooked) eggs, cut in half can be useful. We also find that a large dish of English new potatoes, allowing 100-175g / 4-6oz per person, cooked with fresh mint and served with a knob of butter vanishes in no time. The only guideline to how many you cook is how many you can be bothered to clean. Of course, the ready-prepared new potatoes sold in good supermarkets will lighten your load. A simple Leaf Salad can be made by combining 1/2 head frisée lettuce, 1 head crisp lettuce, such as Cos (Romaine), 1 coloured leaf lettuce, such as Oak Leaf, and 1 small head of Iceberg lettuce and the dressing for Garlicky Green Salad (see page 24), but omitting the garlic.

Strawberry Ice Cream is an ideal alternative for the traditional fresh strawberries and cream. Helge Rubinstein and Sheila Bush's recipe from *Ices Galore* is unsurpassed. In case it is not practical to store ice cream, serve a trifle, following the recipe for Apricot Sherry Trifle (see page 60), but substitute fresh raspberries for the apricots, raspberry jam for the apricot jam and fresh orange juice for the apricot juice.

COLD BAKED GAMMON (FARM HAM)
WITH SUGAR AND CLOVES

SERVES 25 PLUS

8.25-9kg / 18-20lb gammon
(farm ham)
100g / 4oz / ½ cup Demerara
(medium-brown grainy) sugar
approximately 30 whole cloves to
cover leg

A whole gammon (farm ham) weighs 8.25-9kg / 18-20lb. We are very lucky living in Wiltshire – the local gammon is lean and the flavour outstanding. Our butcher bones and rolls the leg, which makes handling and carving much easier. However, a gammon on the bone, resting on a china stand is very spectacular as part of a buffet. A large pot is essential when cooking it on the bone. We use an old aluminium fish kettle with a domed lid that measures 42.5 × 27.5 × 17.5cm / 17 × 11 × 7in. A preserving pan is not deep enough.

Ask the butcher to tie some string tightly round the wide part of the leg so it can be slipped easily into a boiling bag, which a good butcher will supply. The bag protects the gammon while it boils; however, if a bag is not available, ensure that it simmers very gently. The *total* cooking time is 15-20 minutes per 450g / 1lb, plus 15 minutes extra, from the moment it boils.

Soak the gammon (farm ham) in a big bowl under gently running cold water for 24 hours. Dry it and put it into the boiling bag. Squeeze out as much air as possible and tie it up tightly with string. Immerse it in water and bring it to the boil, then lower the heat and simmer the gammon for half the total cooking time (see above). Then lift the gammon on to a wooden board placed conveniently near the sink. There will be a fair amount of liquid in the bag which will ooze out when it is opened. Pierce the bag and allow the liquid to run into the sink before removing the contents.

Preheat the oven to 180°C / 350°F / Gas Mark 4. Cover the gammon tightly with foil and bake it for the remaining cooking time. Thirty minutes before the end remove the foil and strip off the skin, loosening it with the point of a knife. It should come away from the fat easily. Score the fat in a criss-cross pattern, forming squares of about 2.5cm / 1in. Push 1 clove into all 4 corners of each square, then press the sugar evenly all over the gammon. Attach a piece of foil on to the cut surface of the leg, fixing it in place with wooden cocktail sticks (tooth picks); this stops it from drying out too much. Increase the oven temperature to 220°C / 425°F / Gas Mark 7. Put the gammon back in the oven to bake for the last 30 minutes, or until nutty brown.

CUMBERLAND SAUCE

SERVES 8–12
make double the quantity for
25 people
*pared rind and juice of 3
large oranges
pared rind and juice of 2
large lemons
450g / 1lb / 1⅓ cups good-quality
redcurrant jelly
2 heaped tsp Dijon mustard
1 tsp ground ginger
175ml / 6fl oz / ¾ cup port
3 tbsp arrowroot
cold water, to mix
freshly ground black pepper*

Redcurrant preserves can be traced back to the early part of the eighteenth century. The combination of redcurrant jelly and port came somewhat later and originated in Germany where it was served with boars head. Cumberland sauce is an English version and is an excellent accompaniment for cold meats and pies.

Although Elizabeth David in *Spies, Salt and Aromatics in the English Kitchen* suggests that no cornflour (cornstarch) or other thickening should be added, we prefer a slightly thicker sauce. Our version is as follows.

Snip the orange and lemon rinds (peels) with a pair of scissors into fine *julienne* strips and put them in a saucepan with enough cold water to cover. Bring to the boil, then lower the heat and simmer for 10 minutes.

Drain and rinse the strips well in cold water, then drain again and put aside. Put the redcurrant jelly, mustard, ginger, a little pepper and the orange and lemon juice into a saucepan. Stir the mixture over low heat until the redcurrant jelly melts, then add the port and bring it all to the boil.

Meanwhile, blend the arrowroot with a little cold water until smooth. Ladle a small amount of the hot sauce into the arrowroot mixture. Stir well and add it to the mixture in the saucepan. Bring the sauce back to the boil, then simmer for 8-10 minutes, until it becomes clear and slightly thick, stirring all the time. Add the reserved rind and leave to cool, stirring from time to time to avoid a skin forming. Store in a covered container in the refrigerator. Serve at room temperature.

MAKES 50

oil for greasing the roasting tin (pan)
50 chipolata (link) sausages, separated and pricked with a fork on both sides
about 6 tbsp runny honey
about 25g / 1oz / 7 tbsp fresh parsley finely chopped
about 25g / 1oz / 8 tbsp fresh chives finely chopped
about 25g / 1oz / 7 tbsp fresh thyme, leaves, stripped from the stalks (stems)

SAUSAGES BAKED IN HONEY AND HERBS

A sophisticated version of the ever-popular grilled sausage.

Preheat the oven to 220°C / 425°F / Gas Mark 7. Brush the base of a roasting tin (pan) with a little oil. Place the sausages in it and bake for 15 minutes. Shake from time to time to brown the sausages evenly. Brush the sausages well with honey and bake for a further 10-15 minutes, until cooked through. Put all the herbs on a flat dish and mix together well. Roll the hot sausages in the herbs, pressing the herbs in lightly. Serve warm or cold.

SMOKED HADDOCK, LEEK AND TOMATO FLAN (QUICHE)

SERVES 8-12

make 2 flans (quiches) for 25 people
*shortcrust pastry
(piecrust dough) (see method)
350g/12oz smoked haddock fillet,
cut into manageable pieces if large
1 bay leaf
5 whole black peppercorns
1 tbsp olive oil
1 large clove garlic, peeled and finely
chopped
¾ tsp fennel seeds
2 leeks, trimmed, thinly sliced and
well rinsed
450g/1lb tomatoes, peeled (see
method) and roughly chopped, or
400g/14oz can peeled tomatoes,
roughly chopped
¼-½ tsp cayenne pepper
4 medium eggs, lightly beaten
150ml/¼ pint/⅔ cup sour cream
175g/6oz/1½ cups Cheddar
cheese, grated*

For a round fluted tart tin (pan) with a removable base, 25cm/10in in diameter and 2.5cm/1in deep. To peel tomatoes, immerse them briefly in some boiling water. Pierce the skin with the point of a knife and pull it away. This should be easy to do if the tomatoes have been in the water long enough.

Make the pastry dough as for Bakewell Tarts (see page 54), using 225g/8oz/2 cups plain white (all-purpose) flour, 100g/4oz/8 tbsp butter and 1 small egg instead of the water. Wrap in greaseproof (waxed) paper and leave to rest in the refrigerator for 30 minutes. Roll out the pastry dough on a lightly floured surface, line the tart tin and prick the base with a fork. Return to the refrigerator.

Meanwhile, rinse the fish in cold water and put it in a shallow pan with the bay leaf, peppercorns and enough cold water to just cover. Simmer for about 10 minutes or until tender and the fish flakes easily if tested with the tip of a knife. Remove the fish with a slotted fish slice (pancake turner), skin it and roughly flake it, removing any bones.

Preheat the oven to 190°C/375°F/Gas Mark 5. Heat the oil in a heavy-based saucepan and gently fry the garlic, fennel seeds and leeks until softened, stirring from time to time. Add the tomatoes and cayenne pepper (no salt), stir well and simmer, uncovered, for 5 minutes. Remove the pan from the heat and leave it to cool a little. Combine the eggs and sour cream, then stir them into the leek and tomato mixture. Sprinkle half the grated cheese over the pastry case (tart shell), then cover it with the flaked fish. Pour over the leek and tomato mixture and sprinkle the rest of the cheese on top. Bake for 35 minutes. Serve warm or cool.

COLD CHICKEN WITH LEMON SAUCE

SERVES 25

as part of a large buffet
3 × 1.8kg / 4lb oven-ready chickens
salt
3 medium onions, peeled
9 whole black peppercorns
3 bay leaves

FOR THE SAUCE
75g / 3oz / 6 tbsp butter
75g / 3oz / ¾ cup plain white
(all-purpose) flour
salt and freshly ground black pepper
finely grated rind (peel) and juice of
3 lemons
6 egg yolks
900ml / 1½ pint / 3¾ cups single
(light) cream

This recipe is from *Katie Stewart's Cookbook* and is excellent as part of a large buffet. We also serve it on its own with crusty bread and salad, in which case, one 1.8kg / 4lb oven-ready chicken and ⅓ of the sauce quantity is adequate for 6 people.

Wipe the chicken and remove the giblets. Place in a deep pan with salted cold water to cover. Add the onion, peppercorns and bay leaves. Cover and cook gently for 40 minutes, until tender and the chicken's juices run clear. Allow to cool in the liquid for several hours.

Skim the fat from chicken stock and measure 900ml / 1½ pints / 3¾ cups stock for the sauce. Remove the skin and lift the chicken meat from the bones, discarding the skin and bones.

Melt the butter in a saucepan over low heat. Stir in the flour and cook gently for 1 minute. Gradually stir in the chicken stock. Bring to the boil, stirring all the time to make a smooth sauce. Lower the heat and simmer gently for 3-4 minutes. Season with salt and pepper and remove from the heat. Stir in the lemon rind (peel) and juice. Blend the egg yolks with the cream, then stir into the sauce. Check the seasoning, then allow the sauce to cool, stirring occasionally to prevent a skin forming. Cut the chicken into pieces and pour sauce over.

RICE SALAD WITH BLACK (RIPE) OLIVES

SERVES 25

FOR THE SALAD
*900g / 2lb / 4 cups basmati or other
long-grain rice, rinsed several times
in cold water
4 green peppers, cored, de-seeded,
rinsed and cut into small pieces
4 red peppers, cored, de-seeded,
rinsed and cut into small pieces
10 sticks celery, trimmed, rinsed and
thinly sliced
675g / 1½lb / 4 cups sweetcorn
kernels (whole-kernel corn), drained
if canned or cooked, drained and
cooled if frozen
675g / 1½lb small tomatoes,
rinsed and quartered
1 cucumber, rinsed and cut into
small pieces
325g / 12oz / 2½ cups black (ripe)
olives, stoned (pitted) and halved
2 medium onions, peeled and finely
chopped*

FOR THE DRESSING
*350ml / 12fl oz / 1½ cups olive oil
2 tbsp white wine vinegar
2 tsp whole-grain mustard
salt and freshly ground black pepper*

The quantities of vegetables are approximate and can be varied according to choice. The salad is best made several hours before serving.

Fill a very large saucepan with water, add salt and bring it to the boil. Add the rice, stir with a wooden spoon and bring back to the boil. Lower the heat and simmer for 10-15 minutes until tender. The cooking time will vary according to the type of rice used, so test for tenderness after 10 minutes. Drain the rice and drench with cold water, then drain the rice again well and put it in a big bowl. Add the prepared vegetables and olives. Mix the ingredients for the dressing together well or shake them in a screw-top jar. Pour the dressing over the salad while the rice is still slightly warm. Mix the salad thoroughly and test for seasoning. Serve at room temperature.

MIXED BEAN SALAD

SERVES 25

FOR THE SALAD
450g / 1lb frozen whole green beans
*4-6 stalks celery, trimmed, rinsed
and chopped*
*1 bunch spring onions (scallions),
trimmed, rinsed and chopped*
*2 × 400g / 14oz cans red kidney
beans, rinsed and drained*
*2 × 400g / 14oz cans haricot beans,
rinsed and drained*
*2 × 300g / 11oz cans sweetcorn
(whole-kernel corn), drained*
50g / 2oz / 1/3 cup capers, drained
3 tbsp chopped fresh parsley
2 tbsp chopped fresh tarragon

FOR THE DRESSING
300ml / 1/2 pint / 1 1/4 cups olive oil
*300ml / 1/2 pint / 1 1/4 cups
natural yogurt*
*1 clove garlic, peeled and very finely
chopped*
1 tbsp French mustard
1 tbsp lemon juice
salt and freshly ground black pepper

A very easy salad to make in large quantities. It can be eaten straight away, but improves after 1-2 hours.

Cook the whole green beans according to the instructions on the packet (package), then leave them to cool. Cut the beans into 2.5cm/1in lengths. Combine all the salad ingredients in a large bowl. Mix the dressing ingredients together or shake them in a screw-top jar, then pour over the salad and stir well. Serve at room temperature.

WHOLEMEAL (WHOLE-WHEAT) ORANGE BISCUITS (COOKIES)

MAKES 30

*350g / 12oz / 3 cups plain wholemeal
(wholewheat) flour
1 tsp baking powder
175g / 6oz / heaped ¾ cup soft light
brown sugar
175g / 6oz / 12 tbsp butter, cut in
pieces, plus a little extra
finely grated rind (peel) of 2 large
oranges
1 large egg*

Put the flour, baking powder, sugar, butter and orange rind (peel) in a food processor and process until crumbly, then add the egg and process again until a ball of pastry dough is formed. Alternatively, rub or cut the butter into the flour and baking powder until it is crumbly. Stir in the sugar and orange rind (peel), then add the egg and knead the mixture to a smooth dough. Form the dough into 2 rolls, each about 5cm / 2in in diameter, wrap them in greaseproof (waxed) paper and chill them in the refrigerator for about 1 hour, until firm.

Meanwhile, preheat the oven to 180°C / 350°F / Gas Mark 4. Lightly grease 2 baking (cookie) sheets. Cut the dough rolls into thin slices, about 0.3cm / ⅛in thick and place them on the baking sheets. Bake for 15 minutes, until they are golden brown. Transfer to a rack and cool.

STRAWBERRY ICE CREAM

SERVES 25

*550g / 1¼lb / heaped 3 cups caster
(superfine) sugar
225ml / 8fl oz / 1 cup cold water
1.8kg / 4lb strawberries, gently
rinsed and hulled
4 tbsp lemon juice
4 tbsp orange juice
1.2 litres / 2 pints / 5 cups single
(light) cream*

Make a syrup by putting the sugar and water in a saucepan over medium heat. Stir to dissolve the sugar in the water, then bring it to the boil, lower the heat and simmer for 3 minutes. Pour the syrup into a large bowl and allow it to cool. Meanwhile, purée the strawberries in a food processor or blender. Add the strawberry purée to the syrup with the orange and lemon juice. Stir in the cream, then transfer it to a freezerproof plastic container and freeze for a few hours, until mushy. Process the mixture thoroughly in a food processor or blender or beat in an electric mixer. Return to the freezer until completely frozen, preferably overnight. Take the ice cream out of the freezer 1 hour before serving and leave in the refrigerator. Transfer it to a shallow dish.

SPUR OF THE MOMENT PICNIC

MENU FOR 1 OR MORE

Tomato and Green Bean Salad

Layered or Filled Loaf, or Cold Omelettes

Bakewell Tarts

Here are some simple ideas that can be quickly assembled for the one fine day of the English summer.

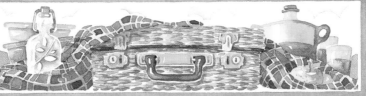

TOMATO AND GREEN BEAN SALAD

SERVES 2

FOR THE SALAD
*225g / 8oz tomatoes, rinsed and
thickly sliced
225g / 8oz frozen green beans,
lightly cooked
2-3 spring onions (scallions),
rinsed, trimmed and finely chopped
1 small clove garlic, peeled and
finely chopped (optional)
chopped fresh parsley*

FOR THE DRESSING
*1 tbsp good-quality olive oil
few drops white wine vinegar
¼ tsp grainy mustard
salt and freshly ground black pepper*

Arrange the tomatoes and beans in a shallow dish or container with the spring onions (scallions), garlic and parsley on top.

Combine all the dressing ingredients or shake them up in a screw-top jar and pour the dressing over the salad shortly before serving.

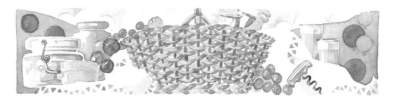

LAYERED LOAF

Split a large, oblong uncut loaf of bread horizontally into several equal pieces, each no thicker than 1cm / ½in. Cut off the top and bottom crusts. Butter the bread on each side and reassemble the loaf, with different fillings between each layer, such as soft or grated cheese, pâtés or dips, chopped hard-boiled (hard-cooked) eggs or canned tuna fish mashed with mayonnaise. Wrap the loaf tightly in foil and refrigerate for at least 1 hour. Trim off the crust ends, then cut the loaf vertically into thick slices. Wrap the slices individually in foil.

FILLED LOAF

Cut a French bread stick into pieces about 20cm / 8in long, or use 1 short stick per person. Cut off both ends and remove the soft bread from the insides. Fill each stick with a mixture of chopped cold meats, hard-boiled (hard-cooked) eggs, salads, gherkins (pickles) and olives combined with a little mayonnaise or similar.

COLD OMELETTES

SERVES 1

½ tbsp butter
½ tbsp corn oil
½ small onion, peeled and thinly sliced
50g / 2oz / ⅔ cup button mushrooms, wiped and thinly sliced
2 large eggs
25g / 1oz smoked salmon, cut into strips
1 tbsp chopped fresh basil or parsley
1 tbsp cold water
salt and freshly ground black pepper

It was our friend Deirdre Connolly Levi, who first suggested that cold omelettes were perfect, simple picnic food. Any combination of ingredients such as diced bacon, ham, salami, cooked potatoes, peppers, peeled tomatoes, cheese, and so on, can be added instead of the smoked salmon, mushroom and onion suggested below. Make one omelette per person in a small heavy-based frying pan (skillet) that measures approximately 20cm / 8in in diameter. Carry them in a food box with greaseproof (waxed) paper or foil between each one.

Preheat the grill (broiler). Melt the butter with the oil in the frying pan (skillet), then gently fry the onion until softened, but not browned. Stir in the mushrooms and cook briefly. Meanwhile, put the eggs into a bowl and break them up with a fork. Mix in the smoked salmon, basil or parsley, water and some seasoning. Turn up the heat under the frying pan, then pour in the egg mixture, stirring to distribute the ingredients fairly evenly. Reduce the heat and cook for 2-3 minutes, until the underside of the omelette is browned and the eggs are fairly set. Place the frying pan (skillet) under the grill and cook for another 2-3 minutes, until risen and golden on top. Loosen the edges with a palette knife (spatula), then slide the omelette on to a plate and leave it to cool.

BAKEWELL TARTS

FOR THE PASTRY
*100g / 4oz / 1 cup plain white
(all-purpose) flour
50g / 2oz / 4 tbsp butter, cut
into pieces
about 1½ tbsp very cold water*

FOR THE FILLING
*4 tbsp good-quality raspberry jam
50g / 2oz / 4 tbsp butter, at room
temperature
50g / 2oz / ¼ cup caster
(superfine) sugar
few drops almond essence (extract)
1 medium egg
50g / 2oz / ½ cup ground almonds
(ground blanched almonds)
3 tbsp flaked (slivered) almonds*

Makes 4 small tarts in round fluted tart tins (pans) with removable bottoms that measure 10cm / 4in diameter, or 1 tart in a 20cm / 8in round fluted tart tin (pan) with a removable base.

To make the pastry, put the flour and butter into a food processor and process until crumbly. Add the water and process until a smooth ball of pastry dough is formed. Alternatively, rub or cut the butter into the flour, then add the water and lightly knead to a smooth pastry dough. Divide the pastry into 4 pieces, then roll each piece out separately on a lightly floured surface and line the tart tins (pans). Prick the base with a fork, then spread 1 tbsp jam over each and chill about 30 minutes.

Make the filling by putting the butter, sugar, almond essence (extract), egg and ground almonds into a food processor and processing until smooth. Alternatively, cream the butter, sugar and almond essence together, then lightly beat the egg and add it a little at a time, beating thoroughly. Stir in the ground almonds.

Meanwhile, preheat the oven to 200°C / 400°F / Gas Mark 6. Divide the filling between the 4 tins and smooth the surfaces. Sprinkle with the flaked (slivered) almonds and bake for 20 minutes (or 30 minutes for a large tart), until risen and golden. Serve warm or cool.

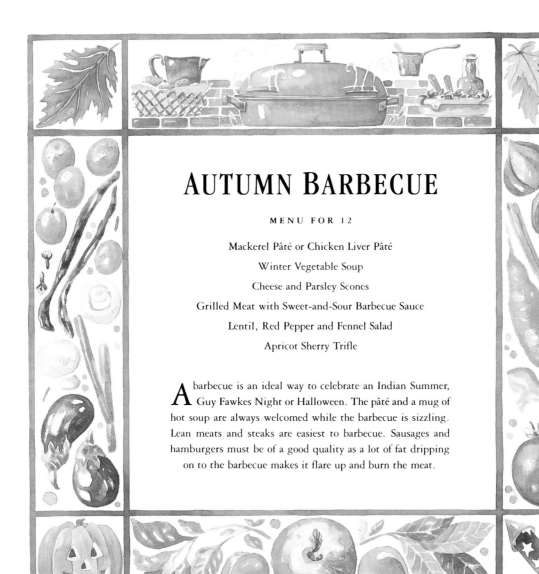

AUTUMN BARBECUE

MENU FOR 12

Mackerel Pâté or Chicken Liver Pâté

Winter Vegetable Soup

Cheese and Parsley Scones

Grilled Meat with Sweet-and-Sour Barbecue Sauce

Lentil, Red Pepper and Fennel Salad

Apricot Sherry Trifle

A barbecue is an ideal way to celebrate an Indian Summer,
Guy Fawkes Night or Halloween. The pâté and a mug of
hot soup are always welcomed while the barbecue is sizzling.
Lean meats and steaks are easiest to barbecue. Sausages and
hamburgers must be of a good quality as a lot of fat dripping
on to the barbecue makes it flare up and burn the meat.

CHICKEN LIVER PÂTÉ

SERVES 12

*225g / 8oz / 2 sticks butter, cut
into pieces
1 large onion, peeled and finely
chopped
2 cloves garlic, peeled and crushed
450g / 1lb chicken livers,
well trimmed and cut into
even-sized pieces
2 tbsp brandy
salt and freshly ground black pepper*

This is a rich and luxurious pâté which should be eaten with dry toast, crusty bread or very plain savoury biscuits (crackers). Sweet-and-sour pickled gherkins are a good accompaniment and can be handed round with the pâté. Cut off any discoloured parts of the livers before cooking them, otherwise the finished dish will have a slightly bitter flavour.

Melt half the butter in a large heavy-based frying pan (skillet). Fry the onion and garlic gently until they are soft but not brown. Turn up the heat and add the livers to the pan, stirring them until they are brown on the outside and a little pink on the inside but without any blood running from them. Put the livers and buttery juices, scraping up any pieces that have stuck to the pan, into a food processor or blender. Add the remaining butter, brandy and plenty of seasoning, then process until smooth. Transfer the mixture to an earthenware or china dish and cool. Chill the pâté until firm but serve at room temperature.

MACKEREL PÂTÉ

SERVES 12

*450g / 1lb smoked mackerel fillets,
skinned and any small bones removed
275g / 10oz / 1¼ cups curd cheese
(medium-fat cream cheese)
2 cloves garlic, peeled and crushed
juice of 1 large lemon
few drops Worcestershire Sauce
freshly ground black pepper
2-3 bay leaves*

This pâté is very easy to make and is a good standby for a gathering.

Put all the ingredients, except the bay leaves, in a food processor or blender and blend together thoroughly. Check the seasoning and add a little more lemon juice or Worcestershire Sauce to taste. Put into a serving dish, flatten the surface with a knife and lightly press the bay leaves on top. Chill.

WINTER VEGETABLE SOUP

SERVES 12

3 tbsp olive oil
1 large onion, peeled and chopped
1 large clove garlic, peeled and crushed
350g / 12 oz / 1½ cups white cabbage, trimmed and shredded
350g / 12oz / 2⅓ cups potatoes, peeled and coarsely grated (at the last minute)
225g / 8oz / 2 cups carrots, peeled and grated
400g / 14oz can baked beans
400g / 14oz can peeled tomatoes
1 bay leaf
1 tbsp Worcestershire Sauce
3 litres / 5 pints / 3 quarts chicken or vegetable stock
350g / 12oz frozen peas
50g / 2oz fine Italian egg vermicelli
salt and freshly ground black pepper
about 5 tbsp Italian pesto sauce (optional)

This is a version of minestrone soup made by our dear family friend, Theo Chadwick. He made vast quantities and froze them in batches at a time when this was quite a new innovation. His wife Thelma and their three boys loved sprinkling grated Cheshire cheese over it, which is delicious when it melts in the hot soup. Any other full-flavoured hard cheese, such as Cheddar, works just as well. Alternatively, serve soup with Cheese and Parsley Scones (see page 58). Use a heavy-based saucepan with lid holding 6 litres / 10 pints / 8½ quarts.

Heat the oil in a large heavy-based saucepan and fry the onion and garlic until softened but not browned. Add the cabbage, potatoes and carrots and coat them in oil, then stir in the beans, tomatoes, bay leaf and Worcestershire Sauce. Season and cook the mixture over low heat for a few minutes, stirring frequently. Add the chicken or vegetable stock and stir again. Cover the pan and cook on a low heat for 1¼ hours.

Mix in the peas and bring it back to the boil. Add the vermicelli, bring it all back to the boil again, then lower the heat and simmer for a final 15 minutes. Remove the bay leaf. Stir in the pesto sauce and serve.

CHEESE AND PARSLEY SCONES

MAKES ABOUT 20

*450g / 1lb / 4 cups plain white
(all-purpose) flour*
4 tsp baking powder
*100g / 4oz / 1 stick butter, cut into
pieces, plus a little extra*
*2 eggs, lightly beaten and enough
cold milk to make 300ml / ½ pint /
1¼ cups liquid*
*200g / 8oz / 2 cups strong Cheddar
cheese, grated, plus a little extra*
4 tbsp chopped fresh parsley

Preheat the oven to 220°C / 425°F / Gas Mark 7.

Put the flour, baking powder and butter into a food processor and process until crumbly, then add the liquid and process again to make a soft, smooth dough. Mix in the cheese and parsley by switching the processor on in several short bursts. Alternatively, put the flour and baking powder in a large mixing bowl, and rub or cut in the butter, then stir in the cheese and parsley. Mix in the liquid and knead lightly to form a soft, smooth dough.

Roll out the dough on a lightly floured surface until about 1cm / ½in thick, then cut into 5cm / 2in rounds with a floured pastry cutter. Place the scones on a lightly greased baking (cookie) sheet, brush the tops lightly with milk and sprinkle a little more grated cheese over each of them. Bake for 12-15 minutes, until golden brown. Cool on a wire rack. These are best served warm.

SERVES 12

FOR THE SALAD

*450g / 1lb / heaped 2½ cups whole
green lentils*
*225g / 8oz / 1⅓ cups fennel, rinsed,
trimmed and chopped*
*2 large red peppers, cored, de-seeded,
rinsed and chopped*
*2 large oranges, peeled
(seeds) removed, sliced and cut into*

LENTIL, RED PEPPER AND
FENNEL SALAD

Rinse the lentils, put them in a saucepan with plenty of cold water to cover, then bring them to the boil. Boil them hard for 10 minutes, then skim the liquid, lower the heat and simmer the lentils, covered, for 25-30 minutes, until they are tender but not mushy. Leave them in a sieve (strainer) to drain very well until they are cool. Combine the

small pieces, reserving any juice for
the dressing
1 bunch spring onions (scallions)
rinsed, trimmed and chopped
100g / 4oz / ⅔ cup black (ripe)
olives, stoned (pitted) and halved

FOR THE DRESSING
300ml / ½ pint / 1¼ cups olive oil
75ml / ⅛ pint / ⅓ cup orange juice
1 tbsp French mustard
1 clove garlic, peeled and very finely
chopped
lemon juice, to taste (see below)
salt and freshly ground black pepper

MAKES ABOUT
600ml / 1 pint / 2½ cups
2 tbsp corn oil
5 tbsp soft brown sugar
100g / 4oz / ½ cup tomato
purée (paste)
300g / 10oz / heaped 1 cup
tomato ketchup
¼-½ tsp Tabasco sauce or to taste
2 tbsp soy (soya) sauce
juice of 1 large lemon
freshly ground black pepper

cooked lentils, fennel, red peppers, oranges, spring onions (scallions) and olives in a large bowl. Mix the dressing ingredients together or shake them in a screw-top jar, adding some lemon juice to taste if the orange juice is very sweet. Pour the dressing over the salad just before serving and stir lightly.

SWEET-AND-SOUR BARBECUE SAUCE

This sauce is suitable for any kind of barbecued or grilled (broiled) meat, fish or vegetables. Brush it all over from about half-way through the total cooking time through to the end.

Heat the oil in a heavy-based saucepan. Add the sugar and stir over medium heat for a few minutes, then add the remaining ingredients, adjusting the seasoning to taste. If not using at once, store in the refrigerator for up to 1 week.

APRICOT SHERRY TRIFLE

SERVES 12

900g / 2lb fresh apricots, halved and
stoned (pitted), or 2 × 400g / 14oz
cans apricot halves in juice
300ml / ½ pint / 1¼ cups cold water
150ml / ¼ pint / ⅔ cup white wine
100g / 4oz / ½ cup caster
(superfine) sugar
1 cinnamon stick
1 strip each lemon and orange
rinds (peels)
16 trifle sponges or
about 400g / 14oz dry sponge cake
175g / 6oz / ½ cup good-quality
apricot jam
225ml / 8fl oz / 1 cup sherry
300ml / ½ pint / 1¼ cups
whipping cream
50g / 2oz / ½ cup flaked (slivered)
almonds, toasted to decorate

FOR THE CUSTARD

8 large eggs, at room temperature
50g / 2oz / ¼ cup caster
(superfine) sugar
600ml / 1 pint / 2½ cups milk
600ml / 1 pint / 2½ cups single
(light) cream
vanilla pod (bean)

We always shied away from cooking a real egg custard because the failure rate was excessive. Since we acquired a stainless steel Hackmann triple steamer egg custards are not a problem. Make the trifle a day before it is to be used and serve chilled. This recipe requires a china or glass bowl which holds about 4 litres / 7 pints / 4 quarts.

Put the fresh apricots, water, wine, caster (superfine) sugar, cinnamon stick and the lemon and orange rinds (peels) into a saucepan. Bring slowly to the boil, then lower the heat and simmer for about 5 minutes, or until the apricots are just tender. Strain, reserving 225ml / 8fl oz / 1 cup juice and leave to cool. Alternatively, strain the canned apricots and reserve 225ml / 8fl oz / 1 cup of the juice. Meanwhile, split the trifle sponges lengthways, spread with the jam and reassemble them. Break them in half and put them in the bottom of a large dish. Slice the apricots and arrange them over the sponges, then dribble over the sherry, followed by the reserved apricot juice evenly over the top. Press the apricots and sponges down lightly with the back of a spoon to smooth the surface.

To make the custard, put the eggs and sugar in a large bowl and mix them well with a fork. Combine the milk and cream and heat them with the vanilla pod (bean) in the top of a double boiler or in a bowl over a pan of barely simmering water. Stir a little of the hot milk and cream into the egg mixture, then pour it all back into the double boiler and stir continuously until it thickens and has a creamy consistency but do not let it get near boiling point. Remove the vanilla pod, then pour the custard over the sponge and apricot base. Cool, then cover and chill overnight. When ready to serve, lightly whip the cream, and cover the custard with it. Scatter the almonds on top just before serving.

FESTIVE AUTUMN PICNIC

MENU FOR 12

Cold Aubergine (Eggplant) Pâté with Tomato and Basil Sauce

Venison Casserole with Wine and Kumquats

Garlicky Green Salad (see Festive spring menu on page 19)

Onion Bread

French Apple Tart

A transportable feast with an autumnal flavour. Ideal for a race meeting or a house party as all the dishes can be prepared well in advance.

COLD AUBERGINE (EGGPLANT) PÂTÉ

SERVES 6

make 2 pâtés for 12 people
1kg / 2¼lb aubergines (eggplants),
peeled with a potato peeler and cut
into 0.5-1cm / ¼-½in slices
olive oil
1 tbsp dried mixed herbs (Italian
Seasoning)
100g / 4oz / 1 stick butter, melted
150ml / ¼ pint / ⅔ cup double
(heavy) cream
1 medium egg
1 clove garlic, peeled and thinly
sliced
salt and freshly ground black pepper
juice of ½ lemon
Cold Tomato Sauce with Basil and
White Wine to serve

A delicious recipe from our neighbour, Penny Rose. For a 900g / 2lb loaf tin (bread pan) that measures 11 × 21 × 6.25 cm / 4¼ × 8¼ × 2½in.

Arrange the aubergine (eggplant) slices on some large plates and sprinkle them *lightly* all over with salt. Leave them to sweat for 1 hour, then dry the surfaces of the aubergine (eggplant) and the plates with absorbent kitchen paper (paper towels). Turn the slices over, salt the other sides and leave them for another hour then dry the second sides well.

Preheat the oven to 180°C / 350°F / Gas Mark 4. Brush 2 baking (cookie) sheets with oil. Arrange the aubergine slices on the baking sheets and brush the slices with a little more oil. Sprinkle the herbs and some pepper on top and bake for 30 minutes, or until the aubergine slices are tender.

Reduce the oven temperature to 160°C / 325°F / Gas Mark 3.

Put the aubergines, butter, cream, egg, garlic, lemon juice and some pepper (no salt) into a food processor or blender and purée. Line the loaf tin (bread pan) with foil, pour in the aubergine mixture and cover with another piece of foil. Bake in a *bain marie* for 3-4 hours, until the tip of a knife or skewer inserted into the centre comes out clean. Leave in the tin to cool, then turn out, cover and chill in the refrigerator. To serve, cut into thick slices and spoon a little of the sauce on the side.

COLD TOMATO SAUCE WITH BASIL AND WHITE WINE

SERVES 12
1 tbsp olive oil
1 onion, peeled and finely chopped
2 cloves garlic, peeled and finely
chopped
900g / 2lb ripe tomatoes, peeled (see
Smoked Haddock, Leek and Tomato
Flan (Quiche) on page 46) and
roughly chopped
1 tbsp tomato purée (paste)
1 tbsp sugar
3 tbsp dry white wine
2 tbsp chopped fresh basil, or
1½ tsp dried
salt and freshly ground black pepper

Heat the oil in a heavy-based saucepan, and fry the onion and garlic over gentle heat until they are softened but not browned.

Mix in the tomatoes, tomato purée (paste), sugar and some seasoning and simmer, uncovered, for about 10 minutes, until the tomatoes are soft. Leave to cool, then add the wine. Purée the tomato mixture in a food processor or blender, then sieve it. Add the basil and chill in the refrigerator.

VENISON CASSEROLE WITH WINE AND KUMQUATS

SERVES 12

*2.25kg / 5lb stewing venison,
well trimmed and cut into
2.5cm / 1in cubes
50g / 2oz / ½ cup plain white
(all-purpose) flour
salt
3 tbsp olive oil
450g / 1lb shallots or small
onions, peeled
3 tbsp chopped fresh thyme, or
2 tsp dried
12 kumquats, rinsed, cut in half
and pips (seeds) removed
300ml / ½ pint / 1¼ cups beef stock
(optional)
225g / 8oz / 3 cups button
mushrooms, wiped and trimmed
225g / 8oz / ⅔ cup redcurrant jelly*

FOR THE MARINADE

*7 whole cloves
1 large onion, peeled
3 large cloves garlic, peeled and
finely chopped
3 bay leaves
2 heaped tbsp preserved green
peppercorns, well drained
450g / 1lb / 3 cups carrots, peeled and
cut into matchstick strips
1 bottle dry red wine*

Put the venison into a large dish. Make the marinade by pushing the cloves into the onion, and adding it to the meat with the garlic, bay leaves, peppercorns and carrots. Pour over the wine, stir, cover and leave to marinate in a cool place for 24 hours, stirring occasionally. Preheat the oven to 160°C / 325°F / Gas Mark 3. Strain and reserve the marinade. Remove the meat and put it on some absorbent kitchen paper (paper towels). Discard the onion and cloves, but reserve the other flavourings. Put the flour with some salt in a shallow dish, and roll the meat in it to coat it lightly.

Heat the oil in a heavy-based frying-pan (skillet). Brown the meat quickly and transfer it to a large flameproof casserole. Fry the shallots or small onions briefly, then add the garlic, carrots and peppercorns from the marinade, together with the thyme. Coat them all in the oil and meat juices and fry them for a few minutes over a medium heat, then add them to the meat. Pour the reserved marinade into the frying pan (skillet) and bring it to the boil scraping up any pieces of meat that have stuck to the base. Add this together with the kumquats and bay leaves from the marinade to the casserole. Stir thoroughly and bring back to the boil, then cover and cook for about 1½ hours. Add the mushrooms, stir in the redcurrant jelly, check the seasoning and add some stock if necessary. Stir well and cook for another 30 minutes or until the meat is tender.

ONION BREAD

MAKES 1 LARGE LOAF

*450g/1lb/4 cups plain wholemeal
(whole-wheat) flour
450g/1lb/4 cups strong (hard)
white bread flour
1/2 tsp salt
1 × 6-7g/1/4oz sachet (envelope)
easy-blend (quick-rising) yeast
50g/2oz/4 tbsp butter, cut
into pieces
150ml/1/4 pint/2/3 cup milk
300ml/1/2 pint/1 1/4 cups cold water
1 large onion, peeled and chopped
2-3 tbsp olive oil
1 large onion, peeled and thinly
sliced*

Put the flours, salt and yeast into a food processor. Melt the butter in the milk and bring it to the boil, then add the cold water. Pour the warm liquid into the dry ingredients while the processor is running and process until a smooth ball of dough is formed. Leave the lid on the processor and put the dough in a warm place for about 1 hour, until it has doubled in size. Alternatively, melt the butter in the liquid as above and add it to the flours, salt and yeast in a large bowl. Knead for a few minutes with a dough hook in an electric mixer or knead the dough by hand until it is smooth and leaves the sides of the bowl clean, cover the bowl with a clean cloth and leave it to rise as above.

Meanwhile, fry the chopped onion in 1 tbsp oil until it is softened, but not browned. Brush a baking (cookie) sheet with a little of the remaining oil. Add the chopped onions to the dough and process or knead it again lightly. Form the dough into a smooth, flat, round shape and put it in the centre of the baking sheet. Cover with a cloth and leave the dough in a warm place to rise again for 45 minutes.

Meanwhile, preheat the oven to 230°C/450°F/Gas Mark 8. Brush the surface of the dough with oil, arrange the onion rings all over the bread, then drizzle a little more oil on top. Bake the bread for 40 minutes, or until the loaf sounds hollow when tapped on the base. Cover the bread with a piece of foil towards the end of the cooking time if the onions seem to be getting too brown. Cool the loaf on a wire rack.

FRENCH APPLE TART

SERVES 8
make 2 tarts to serve 12 or more

FOR THE PASTRY
*225g / 8oz / 2 cups plain white
(all-purpose) flour
100g / 4oz / 1 stick butter
2 tbsp caster (superfine) sugar
1 medium egg*

FOR THE FILLING
*900g / 2lb / heaped 3 cups cooking
apples, peeled, cored and cut into
chunks with peel and cores reserved
175g / 6oz / scant 1 cup caster
(superfine) sugar
25g / 1oz / 2 tbsp butter
1 tbsp water
juice of ½ lemon
4 whole cloves
5-6 small dessert apples, peeled,
cored, quartered and thinly sliced
with peel and cores reserved*

FOR THE GLAZE
*icing (confectioners') sugar, sifted
for dredging
225g / 8oz / heaped 1 cup
granulated sugar
450ml / ¾ pint / scant 2 cups
cold water*

Although this recipe appears to be a rather long haul, it is actually quite easy to make. Guests always think the tart has been made by a professional *pâtissier*, so it is well worth the effort.

Discard any bad pieces of apple, but reserve all the peel and core, immersing them immediately in a big bowl of cold water. Slice the peeled dessert apples straight into a separate bowl of cold water with a little salt in it to prevent the slices from going brown. Glaze the tart at least 1 hour before serving. For a round fluted tart tin (pan) with a removable base 25cm / 10in in diameter and 2.5cm / 1in deep.

Preheat the oven to 200°C / 400°F / Gas Mark 6. Make a pastry dough as for Bakewell Tarts on page 54, mixing the sugar into the flour and butter crumbs and using a medium egg instead of the water. Wrap the pastry dough in greaseproof (waxed) paper and chill it for about 30 minutes. Roll out the pastry dough on a lightly floured surface and use it to line the tart tin (pan). Press the dough well into the fluted edge with your fingertips and prick the base with a fork. Bake blind as for Leek and Broccoli Flan (Quiche) on page 70.

Reduce the oven temperature to 190°C / 375°F / Gas Mark 5. Meanwhile, make the filling. Cook the cooking apple, sugar, butter, water, lemon juice and cloves in a large, heavy-based saucepan over a very gentle heat, stirring from time to time, until the apples are completely soft. Remove the cloves and blend the apple mixture with a fork or balloon whisk to a smooth purée. Leave the purée to cool then spoon it into the cooked pastry case (tart shell).

Rinse the dessert apple slices several times in cold water, then drain them well. Arrange the slices on top of the purée, overlapping each other, in concentric circles starting at the outside edge. Put 4-5 slices of apple together in the centre, standing up to look like a fan-shaped apple quarter. Bake for 35-40 minutes, until the pastry is golden brown and the apple slices are just soft.

Meanwhile, preheat the grill (broiler). Dredge the apple slices with icing (confectioners') sugar then put the tart briefly under the grill so the sugar on the top edges of the apple slices caramelizes to a deep brown. Avoid getting any sugar on the pastry edges. The tart may need turning to caramelize the apples evenly. Watch it carefully, as the sugar can quickly burn. Leave the tart to cool before glazing.

Make the glaze by draining the reserved peel and cores. Then put them in a large, heavy saucepan with 450ml / ¾ pint / scant 2 cups cold water. Bring to the boil, cover and simmer gently for 1 hour. Strain the liquid and measure 300ml / ½ pint / 1¼ cups into a saucepan. Add the granulated sugar, and stir gently over medium heat to dissolve it, then bring it to the boil and boil rapidly for about 10 minutes. Put a few drops of the glaze on a cold saucer and if it wrinkles when you push with your fingertip it is ready. Leave the glaze to cool for a few minutes until it starts to thicken, then spoon it all over the surface of the cooled tart.

SIMPLE WINTER PICNIC

MENU FOR 12

Potted Smoked Salmon

Leek and Broccoli Flan (Quiche)

Beef Casserole with Wine and Olives

Wholemeal (Whole-wheat) Bread with Sunflower Seeds

Leaf Salad with Parsnips and Stilton Toasts

Rhubarb and Ginger Fool

Almond Biscuits (Cookies)

This is an ideal menu for a picnic in the car park (parking lot) at Twickenham. We like to take some Potted Smoked Salmon, or similar, to offer to unexpected friends passing by.

POTTED SMOKED SALMON

SERVES AT LEAST 12

*450g / 1lb smoked salmon bits,
trimmed and cut into small pieces
350g / 12oz / 1½ cups cream cheese
150ml / ¼ pint / ⅔ cup double
(heavy) cream, lightly whipped
50g / 2oz / 4 tbsp butter, cut into
small pieces
2-3 tbsp lemon juice
freshly ground black pepper
a little diced salmon
to decorate (optional)*

Serve this on a wide, shallow dish surrounded by savoury biscuits (crackers) and strips of cucumber. This consistency is best spread with a knife. If you want a dip with crudités, add a little more cream.

Put the smoked salmon in a food processor and process finely. Add all the other ingredients and process again until smooth. Check for seasoning and consistency, then spoon the smoked salmon mixture into a serving dish, decorating the top with a little diced salmon. Cover and chill, but serve at room temperature.

LEEK AND BROCCOLI FLAN (QUICHE)

SERVES 8-12

FOR THE PASTRY

*275g / 10oz / 2½ cups wholemeal
(whole-wheat) flour
150g / 5oz / 10 tbsp butter,
1 medium egg
2-3 tbsp cold water*

This deep quiche is quite substantial and will certainly cut into 12 slices. For Twickenham, however, when unexpected friends may drop by I always make two flans (quiches) as an iron reserve. The second one can always be taken home and frozen if it is not eaten.

For a round fluted tart tin (pan) with a removable base, 25cm/10in × 5cm/2in deep.

To make the pastry dough, put the flour and butter into a food processor and process until crumbly. Add the egg and process again briefly,

FOR THE FILLING
225g / 8oz broccoli, rinsed and
stalks (stems) removed
450g / 1lb leeks, trimmed, sliced in
half lengthways, cut into 2.5 cm /
1in pieces and rinsed well
6 medium eggs
150ml / ¼ pint / ⅔ cup milk
450g / 1lb / 2 cups fromage frais
salt and freshly ground black pepper
175g / 6oz / 2 cups Cheddar
cheese, grated
grated nutmeg

adding enough cold water to form a smooth ball of dough. Alternatively, rub or cut the butter into the flour by hand until it is crumbly. Add the egg and enough cold water to knead the mixture to a smooth ball of dough. Wrap the dough in greaseproof (waxed) paper and chill for about 30 minutes. Preheat the oven to 200°C / 400°F / Gas Mark 6.

Roll out the pastry dough thinly on a lightly floured surface and line the tart tin (pan). Press the dough well into the fluted edge with your fingertips. Prick the base with a fork, and bake the pastry blind by covering it with greaseproof paper and a layer of dry beans or ceramic beads. Put the tin on a baking (cookie) sheet and bake it for 10 minutes. Reduce the oven temperature to 190°C / 375°F / Gas Mark 5. Remove the beans or beads and the paper and continue baking for another 5 minutes. Meanwhile, steam the broccoli for about 8 minutes in a steamer or colander over a pan of boiling water. Add the leeks for the last 5 minutes, or until both vegetables are barely tender. Beat the eggs, milk and some seasoning well into the fromage frais.

Scatter about half the cheese over the pastry, then arrange the broccoli and leeks on top. Gently pour over the egg mixture, then cover the surface with the rest of the cheese and some nutmeg. Bake the flan for 50 minutes, until it is risen and golden. Serve warm or cold.

BEEF CASSEROLE WITH WINE AND OLIVES

SERVES 12

6-8 tbsp olive oil
5 large onions, peeled and thinly sliced
4 large cloves garlic, peeled and crushed
2.5kg / 5½lb stewing (chuck) steak, cut into cubes
900g / 2lb / 6 cups carrots, peeled and cut into matchstick pieces
2 bay leaves
1.2 litres / 2 pints / 5 cups dry red wine
225g / 8oz / 1 cup tomato purée (paste)
175g / 6oz / 1 heaped cup black (ripe) olives, stoned (pitted)
450g / 1lb / 3 cups frozen peas
salt and freshly ground black pepper

Use a heavy-based casserole, with a tight-fitting lid, that holds approximately 5 litres / 8 pints / 5 quarts, or 2 smaller casseroles or flameproof dishes.

Preheat the oven to 130°C / 250°F / Gas Mark 1/2. Cover the base of a large frying pan (skillet) with oil and heat gently. Add the onions and garlic and cook for 5 minutes, stirring occasionally, until the onions are soft but not browned. Put half the mixture aside. Add half the meat to the onions in the pan and cook the mixture on medium heat, stirring occasionally to prevent sticking, until the meat is sealed and slightly browned. Transfer the meat to a large casserole or flameproof dish. Repeat this with the remaining meat and reserved onions and garlic. Leave the meat juices in the frying pan (skillet) and add a little more oil if necessary. Add the carrots and stir until they are well coated with the meat juices and oil. Transfer the carrots to the meat mixture in the casserole, scraping up all the remains in the base of the frying pan and adding these to the casserole as well.

Season well with salt and pepper and add the bay leaves. Give the casserole a good stir, cover and cook for 4-5 hours without adding any liquid: the very slow cooking, or sweating, allows all the ingredients' natural juices to come out. When the meat is tender, remove the casserole from the oven, add the wine and stir well. Bring the casserole to the boil, then return it to the oven for a further 30 minutes. Stir in the tomato purée (paste), olives and peas. Bring to the boil again, stir well and check the seasoning. Cook for a final 30 minutes. Remove the bay leaves before serving.

WHOLEMEAL (WHOLE-WHEAT) BREAD WITH SUNFLOWER SEEDS

450g / 1lb / 4 cups plain wholemeal (whole-wheat) flour
225g / ½lb / 2 cups strong (hard) white bread flour
3 tbsp sunflower seeds, plus a few extra
½ tsp salt
1 × 6-7g / ¼oz sachet (envelope) easy-blend (quick rising) yeast
1 tbsp oil, plus extra for the loaf tin (bread pan)
150ml / ¼ pint / ⅔ cup boiling water
300ml / ½ pint / 1¼ cups cold water
milk for glazing

I always take plenty of bread to Twickenham as well as some savoury biscuits (crackers).

This makes enough dough to fill a 900g / 2lb loaf tin (bread pan) that measures 11 × 21 × 6.25cm / 4¼ × 8¼ × 2½in, but it can also be formed into a large flat round or oval and cooked on an oiled baking (cookie) sheet.

Put the flours, sunflower seeds, salt, yeast and 1 tbsp oil into a food processor, taking care not to overload it. Mix the boiling and cold waters together, then, with the machine running add them to the rest of the ingredients. Process until a smooth ball of dough is formed. Leave the lid on the food processor and leave the dough in a warm place for about 1 hour, until it doubles in size. Alternatively, combine the ingredients together in a large bowl. Knead them for a few minutes with a dough hook in an electric mixer or knead the dough by hand until it is smooth and leaves the edge of the bowl clean. Cover the bowl with a clean cloth and leave the dough in a warm place to rise as above.

Meanwhile, oil the loaf tin (bread pan) or a baking (cookie) sheet well. Process or knead the dough lightly again, then press it into the prepared tin or shape on the baking sheet. Push the dough down all round the edge for a round-topped loaf. Cover the tin with the cloth and leave the dough in a warm place to rise again for a further 30 minutes.

Meanwhile, preheat the oven to 230°C / 450°F / Gas Mark 8. Brush the surface of the bread dough with a little milk and sprinkle a few sunflower seeds on top, pressing them in lightly to stop them falling off. Bake the bread for 30-40 minutes or as soon as it sounds hollow if tapped on the base. Turn the loaf out on to a wire rack to cool.

LEAF SALAD WITH PARSNIPS AND STILTON TOASTS

SERVES 12

450g / 1lb / 3 cups parsnips, peeled and cut into matchstick strips
salt for blanching
4 large slices bread, toasted
75g / 3oz Stilton cheese
1 large head Iceberg or crisp green lettuce, rinsed and torn into small pieces
1 head Lollo Rosso or Oak Leaf lettuce, rinsed and torn into small pieces
1 large head Raddiccio, rinsed and torn into small pieces
2 bunches watercress, trimmed, rinsed, large stalks (stems) removed and well drained
225g / 8oz black grapes, rinsed, halved and pips (seeds) removed
½ bunch spring onions (scallions), rinsed, trimmed and chopped

FOR THE DRESSING
150ml / ¼ pint / ⅔ cup olive oil
150ml / ¼ pint / ⅔ cup walnut oil
2 tbsp wine vinegar
salt and freshly ground black pepper

This salad is also good served as a starter (appetizer).

Blanch the parsnips in lightly salted boiling water, refresh them in cold water and drain them well. Leave the toast to cool and crispen, then spread with the Stilton. Cut the toast into small triangular pieces, removing the crusts if they are too hard. Assemble the salad by mixing the leaves up in a large, wide bowl, scatter over the grapes, parsnips, Stilton toasts and finally the spring onions (scallions). Mix the salad dressing ingredients together or shake them up in a screw-top jar, then pour over the salad about 30 minutes before serving it.

RHUBARB AND GINGER FOOL

SERVES 12

*1.8kg / 4lb rhubarb, leaves removed,
trimmed, rinsed and cut into
2.5cm / 1in pieces
350g / 12oz / 1¾ cups caster
(superfine) sugar, or more to taste
finely grated rind and juice of 2
large oranges
900ml / 1½ pints / 3¾ cups
sour cream
6 pieces stem (preserved) ginger,
well drained and cut into
matchstick strips*

My husband says there is only one food in the entire world he does not like and that is rhubarb. However, it can be delicious, and this fool proves it. For a picnic it is easiest to serve the fool in individual 7.5cm / 3in ramekins. Wrap the ramekins in foil and leave them in the refrigerator until the last moment. Transport them in a cool box, separated with trimmed down cardboard dividers from an old wine box. Another piece of cardboard, the size of the box and wrapped in foil, helps to divide layers or can act as a lid so the top of the box can be used for other light things.

Preheat the oven to 180°C / 350°F / Gas Mark 4. Mix the rhubarb and caster (superfine) sugar together with the orange rind (peel) and juice in an ovenproof dish. Cover and cook the fruit for 40 minutes, until tender. Strain the rhubarb well and leave it to cool, then purée. Reserve 1 strip of ginger to decorate each fool. Stir the cream and the remaining ginger strips into the rhubarb purée. Test for sweetness, then transfer the fool to individual ramekins or a serving dish, decorate with the reserved ginger and chill.

ALMOND BISCUITS (COOKIES)

MAKES 36

*100g / 4oz / 1 cup plain white
(all-purpose) flour
100g / 4oz / 1 cup ground blanched
almonds
½ tsp baking powder
100g / 4oz / ½ cup caster
(superfine) sugar
100g / 4oz / 1 stick butter, cut into
pieces, plus a little extra
50g / 2oz / ½ cup whole blanched
almonds, chopped
1 medium egg
25g / 1oz / ¼ cup flaked
(slivered) almonds*

Preheat the oven to 180°C / 350°F / Gas Mark 4.

Put the flour, ground (blanched) almonds, baking powder, sugar and butter into a food processor and process until crumbly. Add the chopped almonds and the egg and process in short bursts until a smooth ball is formed; this should keep the chopped almonds intact. Alternatively, put the flour, ground (blanched) almonds and baking powder into a large bowl. Rub or cut in the butter until the mixture is crumbly. Stir in the sugar and the chopped almonds, then add the egg and knead to a smooth dough. Lightly grease 2 or 3 baking (cookie) sheets.

Divide the dough into 3 parts and then each part into roughly 12 pieces. Roll each piece into a ball and place them, well apart, on the baking sheets. Press a piece of flaked (slivered) almond on top of each ball, then bake for 15 minutes, until golden. Transfer the biscuits (cookies) to a wire rack to cool. Store in an air-tight container.

FESTIVE WINTER PICNIC

MENU FOR 12

Pea and Lettuce Soup

Raised Game Pie

Damson Chutney

Chinese Leaf (Pe-tsai) and Orange Salad

Marbled Chocolate Pots with Cognac

Hazlenut Curls (see romantic summer menu on page 39)

A special menu for winter entertaining.

PEA AND LETTUCE SOUP

SERVES 12

50g / 2oz / 4 tbsp butter
450g / 1lb / 3 cups new potatoes,
scraped and diced
2 bunches spring onions (scallions),
trimmed and chopped or 2 medium
onions, peeled and chopped
salt and freshly ground black pepper
1 large head Cos (Romaine) lettuce,
or similar green lettuce rinsed and
torn into pieces
1.2 litres / 2 pints / 5 cups chicken or
vegetable stock
675g / 1½lb / 4½ cups frozen peas
900ml / 1½ pints / 3¾ cups milk
300ml / ½ pint / 1¼ cups single
(light) cream
chopped fresh chives, to serve
50g / 2oz / ½ cup pine nuts, toasted,
to serve (optional)

This soup is delicious served hot or cold.

To toast the pine nuts, put them in a shallow baking tin (pan) under a hot grill (broiler) for 1-2 minutes, shaking them from time to time so they brown evenly.

Melt the butter in a large, heavy-based saucepan, then add the potatoes, onions and some seasoning. Stir well to coat the vegetables in butter, cover and sweat over a low heat for 5 minutes. Add the lettuce, turn up the heat and stir until it has wilted, then add the stock. Bring it to the boil, cover and simmer for 10 minutes. Add the peas, bring it all back to the boil, then lower the heat and simmer for a further 3 minutes. Purée the soup, stir in milk and cream and check the seasoning. Reheat or chill. Sprinkle with chives and pine nuts before serving.

RAISED GAME PIE

It was my husband's love of oval fluted raised game pies, which he tasted as a boy when he visited his school friend John Sykes at the family hotel, which made me take the plunge. Once I got over the trauma of the first one I have never looked back. They are invaluable for a large gathering. A useful tip! Should you mislay the clips which hold the sides of the raised pie tin (pan) together, old fashioned key rings will work splendidly. Various sizes of traditional oval raised pie tins (pans) can be bought from specialist kitchen shops. This recipe will fill a tin approximately 30 × 17.5 × 12.5 cm / 12 × 7 × 5in. A deep, round cake tin with removable base, diameter 25 cm / 10in, and a capacity of 5.1 litres / 8½ pints / 5 quarts, can be used instead, and will certainly be less hassle although not so attractive.

To make the filling, cut the meat off the pheasant and rabbit, reserving the carcass. Remove the sinews and skin, cut it into short thin strips and mix with the venison. Coarsely mince (grind) 100g / 4oz bacon and mix it with the lean and fatty pork and onion. Add the sherry, spices, lemon rind (peel) and parsley and plenty of salt and pepper to the pork mixture. Stretch each of the remaining bacon rashers (slices) with the flat side of a knife blade and put aside.

Meanwhile prepare the jellied stock by putting all the stock ingredients with the reserved carcass and any bones and water into a large stock pot and cover. Bring this to the boil and spoon off the scum, then leave the stock to simmer for 4-5 hours. Remove the bones and strain the stock through muslin (cheesecloth) into a clean pan. Reduce the stock by boiling briskly to 450ml / ¾ pint / scant 3 cups.

To make the pastry crust, preheat the oven to 130°C / 250°F / Gas Mark 1/2. Remember it is very important to keep the pastry dough

FOR THE JELLIED STOCK
2 pig's trotters
1 large carrot, peeled and cut into pieces
2 sticks celery, trimmed, cut into pieces and rinsed
1 peeled onion stuck with 4 cloves
8 whole black peppercorns
2 tsp dried mixed herbs (Italian seasoning)
3 litres / 5 pints / 12½ cups / 3 quarts water
reserved bones from the pheasant and rabbit

warm throughout the preparation. Put the flour and salt into a large mixing bowl and leave to warm through in a very cool oven with the door ajar. Place the fats in a saucepan with the water and bring to the boil. Take the flour out of the oven, make a well in the centre of it and pour in the melted fats, mix it all together well with a wooden spoon to make a pliable dough. Stir in the egg yolks. Cover the dough with a cloth and allow to cool until you can handle it but do not allow it to get too cold.

Divide the dough, leaving one quarter for the lid: this should be set aside and kept warm. Gently roll out the remaining three-quarters dough on a lightly floured surface into an oval shape that is pencil thick. Fold the pastry in half and lower it carefully into the tin (pan). Unfold it and press it gently into the base and quickly push it up the sides of the tin. Press the dough into the fluted indentations and check that the join at the base and sides is well sealed. There must not be any breaks in the dough as the meat juices can run out during baking. Allow the dough to fall somewhat over the top edge. To fill the pie, spread half the sausage-meat over the base, pressing it down well into the joint between the base and sides. Line the sides of the pie with the bacon rashers. Then fill the pie with layers of game, sausage-meat and pork mixture until it is full. Press the meat lightly into the mould and shape the top into a shallow dome. Spoon 2 tbsp jellied stock over the meat. Brush the top edge of the pastry with a little of the beaten egg.

Roll out the remaining pastry and lift it on to the pie with a rolling pin. Press the 2 edges together firmly and trim with a sharp knife. Press the whole edge with the back of a fork to seal the joint, but make sure the pastry does not hang over the rim of the tin as this causes it to break when taking off the sides. Cut a 2.5 cm / 1 in cross in the centre of the pastry lid and fold back the corners to allow the steam to escape during baking. The pastry trimmings can be used to decorate the pie. Leaves and flowers are traditional but any personalized decoration can be fixed to the lid with a little beaten egg. Finally brush egg over the top. Raise the oven temperature to 200°C / 400°F / Gas Mark 6.

Put the pie on a baking (cookie) sheet and bake it for 30 minutes at this temperature, then cover it lightly with foil, lower the heat to 160°C / 325°F / Gas Mark 3 and bake for a further 2¾ hours, removing the foil for the last 30 minutes. Take the pie out of the oven and allow to cool.

While the pie is still just warm, warm the stock, then pour it through the centre hole with a small funnel, taking care to do this very slowly. Keep adding more stock if the pie will absorb it. The stock will fill the gaps left by the meat which shrunk during baking and solidify into a jelly. Leave the pie in a cool place for at least 24 hours before serving. To take to the picnic, leave the pie tin loosely round the pie, wrap in foil and tie a large cloth round to protect it. Transport it in a cardboard wine box.

DAMSON CHUTNEY

1.8kg / 4lb damsons, rinsed
450g / 1lb / 4 cups cooking apples,
peeled, cored and cut into chunks
3 onions, peeled and roughly chopped
225g / 8oz / 2 cups carrots, peeled
and shredded
225g / 8oz / 1½ cups raisins
900g / 2lb / 4½ cups sugar (brown
sugar will make the chutney darker)
1.2 litres / 2 pints / 5 cups malt or
white wine vinegar
2 tbsp salt
2 tsp ground allspice
25g / 1oz fresh root ginger, peeled and
chopped finely
2 tsp ground cloves
1 small dried chilli tied in
muslin (cheesecloth)

The word 'chutney', originally *chatna* or *chitney*, which the British borrowed from the Hindu during the Raj, was apparently first noted as chutney in 1848 by Thackeray in *Vanity Fair*. Chutney is undervalued in international cookery, but the combination of the different fruits, spices and sweet-and-sour additions goes well with a wide range of cold English dishes. There are all too many brands on the supermarket shelves, but made at home and adjusted to personal taste, a family recipe can be evolved and handed from generation to generation. This recipe is from my neighbour Freddie Davison. Damsons, a cultivated form of wild plum, are only available during the early autumn. They can, however, be frozen and the chutney made later. Damsons are difficult to find outside Europe but more familiar plums can be substituted in this recipe. Fills approximately seven 450g / 1lb jars.

Put the damsons in a covered saucepan and cook them slowly until soft. Press the fruit through a colander to remove all the stones (pits). Mix the damson purée together with the apples, onions, carrots, raisins and sugar in a large bowl. Put the vinegar in a stainless steel or enamel-coated saucepan with the salt and spices. Bring this mixture to boiling point, then stir in the fruit and vegetables. Bring back to the boil.

Allow the mixture to simmer for approximately 1 hour, stirring from time to time with a wooden spoon, until it is thick. Remember the chutney thickens more as it cools down. Wash, rinse and dry the jars. Pot the warm chutney and seal with greaseproof (waxed) paper as for jam. Plastic lids can be used, but not metal ones which will be discoloured by the vinegar. Keep the chutney in a cool place for at least 1 month before eating.

SERVES 12

4 large oranges, peeled and all pith and pips (seeds) removed
1 large or 2 small heads, about 1kg / 2¼lb, Chinese leaf (pe-tsai), root end removed, leaves thickly sliced and rinsed
1 small bunch spring onions (scallions), trimmed, rinsed and chopped
poppy seeds (optional)

FOR THE DRESSING
300ml / ½ pint / 1¼ cups corn oil
1 tbsp orange juice
1 tbsp lemon juice
2 tbsp chopped fresh tarragon or 1 tsp dried
salt and freshly ground black pepper

CHINESE LEAF (PE-TSAI) AND ORANGE SALAD

For a picnic, take the dressing separately in the screw-top jar. Cover the salad tightly with foil and assemble it on site.

Slice the oranges horizontally, then cut the slices into smaller pieces.

Assemble the salad by putting Chinese leaf (pe-tsai), oranges and spring onions (scallions) into a large, shallow bowl. Mix all the dressing ingredients together well or shake them in a screw-top jar. Pour over the salad approximately 1 hour before serving. Mix well and sprinkle the poppy seeds on top.

MARBLED CHOCOLATE POTS WITH COGNAC

SERVES 12

*350g / 12oz plain dark (semisweet)
or bitter (bittersweet) chocolate,
broken into pieces
600ml / 1 pint / 2½ cups single
(light) cream
125g / 5oz white chocolate, broken
into pieces
2 medium eggs, lightly beaten in a
measuring jug
vanilla essence (extract)
salt
12 dessertspoonfuls Cognac or
liqueur
(1 dessertspoon = 10ml)*

This recipe was inspired by Helge Rubinstein's Petits Pots au Chocolat in her *Chocolate Book*. It needs to be served in individual glasses or small ramekins and is very rich. Transport to a picnic as for Rhubarb and Ginger Fool on page 75. Serve with Almond Biscuits (cookies) on page 76 or Hazelnut Curls on page 39.

Put the chocolate into a food processor or blender. Heat 400ml / ¾ pint / just over 2 cups cream to the scalding point and pour it over the chocolate. Process to a smooth cream. Add three-quarters of the beaten eggs, a few drops of vanilla essence (extract) and a dash of salt, then process the mixture again briefly. Divide the chocolate cream between the 12 glasses or ramekins.

Alternatively, scald the cream, remove from the heat and stir in the chocolate. Leave for 5 minutes, until the chocolate has melted, then stir until smooth. Stir in the egg, vanilla essence (extract) and salt and beat over a very gentle heat with a wooden spoon until completely smooth. Proceed with the recipe.

Rinse the processor or blender goblet and make a white chocolate cream the same way with the remaining cream and egg. Pour a little of the white chocolate cream into each dark chocolate cream in the dishes and stir briefly with a clean teaspoon until marbled. Take care not to stir too much. Cover and refrigerate for several hours until set. Just before serving, pour a spoonful of Cognac over each chocolate cream.

CHRISTMAS CALLERS

Mulled Wine

Cornish Pasties

Dickens Porridge

There are many gatherings during the run-up to Chrismas when a glass of mulled wine immediately evokes a festive air and is a welcome treat to offer friendly carol singers. Homemade Cornish Pasties are an invaluable stand-by at this busy time of year.

MULLED WINE

FOR ABOUT 16 GLASSES

*1½ litres / 2½ pints / 6¼ cups
dry red wine
500ml / 18fl oz / 2¼ cups cold water
225g / 8oz / heaped 1 cup sugar
pared rind (peel) of 1 lemon
2 cinnamon sticks, 10cm / 4in long
½ tsp grated nutmeg
2 blades mace
3 whole cloves*

A rough, dry red wine is quite acceptable for mulling. The sugar, lemon rind (peel) and spices, plus a long, slow infusion, transform it. We always make the mulled wine in a proportion of three parts wine to one part water. To make a very big quantity, prepare a concentrated brew with the total quantity of sugar, lemon rind (peel) and spices, then pour it into a large container like a tea urn and top it up with the required wine and water mixture. Finally heat it all up slowly and infuse for an hour or as long as possible before serving. The mulled wine must be strained through fine cloth, not just a fine sieve (strainer), to extract the grated nutmeg which makes the wine cloudy. If making a concentrated brew strain it before adding the rest of the wine and water.

Pour the wine and water into a large stainless steel or enamel-coated saucepan. Add the sugar and dissolve it over medium heat, stirring from time to time. Add all the other ingredients and heat the mixture but do not allow it to boil. Cover the pan and infuse the mulled wine over very gentle heat for 3-4 hours, then strain it through a fine cloth into a heatproof bowl. Rinse the pan with cold water and ladle the mulled wine back into it. Reheat the mulled wine before serving. To serve, pour the wine from a warmed, heatproof jug (pitcher) or ladle it into *thick* wine glasses or tumblers.

CORNISH PASTIES

Makes either 4 large or 8 smaller
pasties; for a picnic or packed
lunch the latter is preferable.

FOR THE PASTRY
*450g / 1lb / 4 cups self-raising
(self-rising) flour
100g / 4oz / 1 stick butter, cut into
pieces, plus a little extra for greasing
the baking (cookie) sheet
100g / 4oz / ½ cup lard, cut
into pieces
pinch salt
5-6 tbsp very cold water*

FOR THE FILLING
*450g / 1lb stewing steak, preferably
skirt, trimmed of all fat and sinews
and finely diced
100g / 4oz ox kidney, trimmed and
finely diced (optional: if left out,
adjust quantity of meat or vegetables
accordingly)
225g / 8oz / 1½ cups swedes
(rutabagas), peeled and finely diced
275-300g / 9-10oz / 1¾-2 cups
potatoes, peeled and finely diced
1 large onion, peeled and finely
chopped
1 egg, beaten, or a little milk to
glaze
salt and freshly ground black pepper*

If it had been invented in a French region, the Cornish pasty would be considered a delicacy. It really is, but the mass-produced variety has given it a bad name. You must go back to the roots for an authentic version. My friend, Mary Sloman, whose husband is half Cornish and half Devonian, makes the genuine article. Originally, Cornish pasty was a practical dish to be taken to the field for lunch, wrapped in a clean cloth to keep it warm. Each pasty had the initials of its owner cut into a corner of the half moon shape so individual tastes could be catered for; onion for one, special seasoning for another. If the pasty was not eaten all at once, the owner could then easily find it and finish it later. Like so many traditional English dishes, the pasty could be served in hard times with only vegetables as a filling. Mary's recipes uses ox kidney with the beef which can be left out. These pasties can be eaten cold but are more delicious warm.

The cooked pasties can be frozen, thawed and reheated. However, it is better to freeze the assembled pasty raw providing the meat has *not* been previously frozen. Thaw thoroughly before baking as below.

To make the pastry, put the flour, fats and salt into a food processor and process until crumbly. Add the water gradually and process to form a smooth dough.

Alternatively, rub or cut the fats into the flour and salt until crumbly. Add the water and knead to a smooth dough.

Shape the dough into a neat sausage shape and wrap it in greaseproof (waxed) paper. Allow it to rest in the refrigerator for 2 hours.

To make the filling; mix the beef and kidney together, then divide into 4 or 8 portions. Likewise divide the potatoes, swedes (rutabagas) and onions and place in heaps on 4 or 8 large plates.

Cut the dough into 8 equal-sized pieces. On a lightly floured surface, knead each piece lightly, forming a smooth round ball. Roll out each ball into a round approximately 16.5 cm / 6½in in diameter. Put a layer of diced potatoes in the centre of each pastry round, leaving a clear rim of pastry approximately 3 cm / 1¼in wide. Follow this with a layer of swedes, then the onion and half the meat. Season well and repeat the layers, using up all the filling. Brush the pastry rim with beaten egg or milk. Bring up the 2 sides of the pastry to meet over the top of the filling, making a half moon shape. Press the 2 edges together well, taking care to keep the pastry intact. Crimp the edges to make a scalloped effect, then turn up the 2 ends slightly to stop any juices from running out during baking. Decorate the pasty with pastry trimmings or initials, sticking them on with a little egg or milk. Brush the whole surface well with beaten egg or milk. Repeat with the other portions of pastry and filling. Chill each pasty for at least 15 minutes before cooking. Meanwhile, preheat the oven to 220°C / 425°F / Gas Mark 7. Put the pasties on a lightly greased baking (cookie) sheet and bake for 10 minutes, then lower the heat to 180°C / 350°F / Gas Mark 4 and continue baking for a further 50 minutes. Cool on wire racks.

DICKENS' PORRIDGE

A final word: Cedric Dickens, great grandson of Charles, made this indulgently Dickensian dish to pull us round on the morning after the night before. Make a well in the centre of a steaming hot bowl of porridge. Fill it with a measure of Drambuie, then pour single (light) cream round the edge of the bowl. Sprinkle brown sugar all over the top. It is guaranteed to set you up for the New Year.

Hints

Planning: When planning a picnic for a lot of people it is essential to anticipate approximately how much car boot (trunk) space you will need. Hatchback or estate cars are ideal, but guests may need to come to your aid if you only have an average-size boot.

Location: For a picnic at a big event ask the organizers whether a special parking ticket is required. Some car parks (parking lots) are a long way from the action. Your guests might find a plan useful, but nowadays coloured helium-filled balloons tied to the car are the most chic navigational guide.

Crockery: For a large number of people, the traditional fitted picnic basket is not practical. Very attractive, non-breakable crockery is now available from good supermarkets and stores. For a really upmarket picnic, however, you cannot beat china. If you are a regular picnicker it may be worth investing in a robust set so as not to have heartaches with your best porcelain.

Cutlery and Glass: Plastic knives and forks can be flimsy. Likewise, most paper cups are difficult to manage and not very pleasant to drink out of. A spare set of inexpensive stainless steel cutlery and some solid plastic tumblers or Paris bistro glasses are well worth the investment. Alternatively, glasses can be borrowed from your wine merchant. Keep the boxes for storage or transport.

Tablecloths and Napkins: Paper napkins are liable to blow away and can be a nuisance. A kitchen roll is not elegant but extremely practical, as well as a pack of moist wipes. A luxurious alternative for sticky fingers is a bottle of water and some slices of lemon put in a large bowl. Instead of your best damask tablecloth, a length of country cotton will do, and some hemmed squares to match will be endlessly useful as napkins.

Tables and Chairs: Sitting on the grass with rugs (blankets) is all very well, but the infamous English climate often means that conditions are far from perfect. A folding table and chairs can save the day and in any case a small table for food or drink is very useful.

Containers and Storage: Transport all food that needs to be kept cool in sealed containers or wrapped in foil in a cooling box with freezer packs.

Soups and casseroles can be kept hot in a large vacuum flask. Wide-necked flasks suitable for casseroles are now available in specialist stores. Warm the flask before using by filling it with boiling water, closing it and leaving it to heat through for about ten minutes.

Large wicker picnic hampers, laundry baskets and even shopping baskets are useful for packing. If all else fails, good stout cardboard boxes from the supermarket are indispensable. Pad anything fragile with tea-cloths (dish towels) or pieces of absorbent kitchen paper (paper towels). Take a supply of empty plastic bags for dirty crockery, cutlery and debris.

Salads: The consumption of salad is unpredictable

when serving a lot of people, therefore, the recipes should be used as guidelines only. Some extra prepared ingredients can always be kept available in a plastic bag. In any case, it is best to put the vinaigrette on most leaf salads just before serving. Transport the dressing in a screw-top jar and shake well before pouring over the salad.

Cheese, Bread and Fruit: Prepare a cheese board and some fresh fruit to serve before, after or as an alternative to the pudding: for large numbers two or three big pieces of cheese are preferable to a lot of little ones. One hard, one soft and a blue cheese provide a good choice.

It is always worth taking some good crusty bread on a picnic to eat with the meal or nibble later in the day with a piece of cheese. A tin of savoury biscuits (crackers) should also be included.

Tea and Coffee: A perfectly adequate method of preparing coffee for a picnic is to put good quality instant coffee granules into a heated vacuum flask, filling the flask with freshly boiled water, after warming the flask as described under Containers and Storage then stir it with the handle of a long spoon and top up with more water before closing. Of course, piping hot coffee made from ground coffee beans and poured into a heated flask is better.

Alternatively, flasks of freshly boiled water can be used with coffee filters. This water could also be used to make tea or tisanes from a choice of tea-bags. Freshly boiled water in a kettle over a

Calor gas flame, set up in a sheltered spot (NOT near the car) is best.

Drinks: On the whole we tend to take a fairly robust red wine on a picnic, such as Rioja or Beaujolais. We have overcome the problem of serving red wine too cold by leaving the wine in an airing cupboard overnight and then putting it straight into an insulated box. By the time it has reached the picnic it should be a good temperature for drinking. Similarly champagne or white wines such as Chablis or Sancerre need to be chilled overnight and transported in an insulated box. Unbreakable wine coolers are an advantage on a hot day. Bottled water, beer and soft drinks are essential for a picnic. For boxes of fruit juice a plastic, resealable pourer, available from supermarkets or stores, is helpful. A luxurious touch is to take ice cubes in a wide-necked Thermos jar.

Acknowledgements

We would like to thank everyone who has helped with the book, especially Colin Webb for having faith in us in the first place.

We are also grateful to the following authors and publishers for permission to use extracts from their works: Claudia Roden *A Book of Middle Eastern Food* Penguin Books; Helge Rubinstein *Chocolate* Penguin Books; Helge Rubinstein and Sheila Bush *Ices Galore*; and Katie Stewart *The Katie Stewart Cookbook* Gollancz.

Index